CW00434049

Tail: Medium length, clipped with
tuft of hair to resemble a plume.

Body: Short, strong and well proportioned. Level topline.
Ribs well sprung. Strong loin with moderate tuck-up.

Hindquarters: Hindlegs well
muscled, with good turn of stifle.

Coat: Fairly long, wavy, never curly.
Single coat of soft texture.

Size: Height at withers
25–33 cms (10–13 ins).

Feet: Small, round.

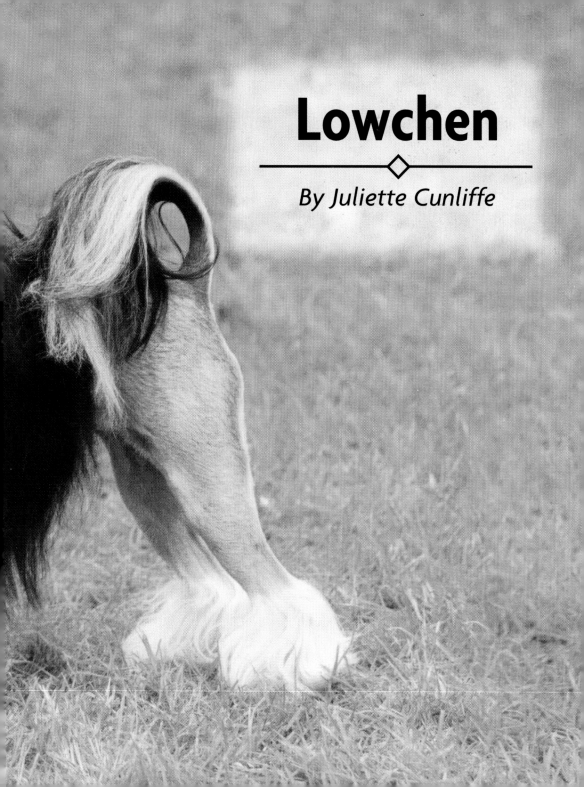

Lowchen

◇

By Juliette Cunliffe

Contents

Lowchen

PUBLISHED IN THE UNITED KINGDOM BY:

INTERPET
PUBLISHING
Vincent Lane, Dorking Surrey RH4 3YX England

ISBN 1-903098-77-7

Photos by Carol Ann Johnson
with additional photos by
Norvia Behling, Mary Bloom, TJ Calhoun,
Carolina Biological Society, Doskocil, Isabelle Français,
James Hayden-Yoav, James R Hayden, RBP, Bill Jonas,
Dwight R Kuhn, Dr Dennis Kunkel, Mikki Pet Products,
Phototake, Jean Claude Revy, Dr Andrew Spielman,
Karen Taylor, Michael Trafford and Alice van Kempen.

Two modern Continental champion representatives of the Lowchen, showing off their impressive coats.

History of the

LOWCHEN

ORIGIN OF THE BREED

The Lowchen is one of many breeds whose history has been rather lost in time, though it would appear that the breed has existed, at least in similar form, for about 2000 years. The earliest known name of the breed is Maltese Lion Dog; to add to the confusion, some Maltese and other breeds were also trimmed in a manner resembling that of the Lowchen we know today. The Lowchen is, in fact, just one of a group of breeds sharing similar ancestry: the Maltese, Bichon Frise, Bolognese, Havanese and Coton de Tulear. Even today, it is sometimes difficult for people unfamiliar with these breeds to distinguish among them. However, the Lowchen clearly stands out as different from the rest because of its characteristic trim, resembling the coat of a lion.

All of the aforementioned breeds come from the same root stock, but each has evolved in its own special way, due in part to whim and fancy and in part to trading routes as they were opened up through the centuries.

Buffon, a famous naturalist of the early nineteenth century, re-named the dog the Bichon Petit Chien Lion (Little Lion Dog) and, probably because of Buffon's own nationality, the French subsequently claimed the Lowchen as French in origin. However, the word *Löwchen* is German, translating to 'Little Lion Dog,' and more accurately being pronounced '*Lerv-chun.*'

Writing in 1907, Robert Leighton claimed that Russia was the original home of the Little Lion Dog, though he believed that, at that time, the breed had no distinctively local habitation. It

'Le Bichon and Le Chien Lion' from Buffon's *Histoire Naturelle,* published in 1798. The name 'Le Bichon' refers to the Bichon Maltese. An early name of the Lowchen was the Maltese Lion Dog.

could, he said, 'just as often be found in Germany or in Holland as in any other country,' noting Mme M de Connick of Dieghem as one of only a few owners who then bred Lion Dogs with success.

With reference to Leighton's comment about the breed just as easily being found 'in any other country,' we know that the Lowchen also enjoyed certain popularity in Italy, Spain and France, even as early as the sixteenth century.

Leighton wondered why this particular breed had not become fashionable, for he described it as an active, well-proportioned dog 'with a winning disposition.' It then weighed only around 2 kgs (a little over 5 lbs) and its long, wavy coat could be almost any colour, but white, lemon and black were preferred. Some such dogs were parti-coloured. Leighton was one of only a few canine writers who imparted any information about this rather

Today's Lowchen is a fashionable, affectionate dog, whose popularity is growing in the UK, the USA and the Continent.

special and unusual breed, telling his readers that the name came from 'the fashion of clipping the coat from the shoulders to the tuft of the tail, leaving a profuse mane which gives the appearance of a lion in miniature.'

THE BREED DESCRIBED IN 1904

In 1894 Count Henry van Bylandt compiled a book initially for an exclusively Dutch readership; by 1904, it had been extended to cover four languages. This made it one of the most wonderfully informative books about dogs that has ever been written. In 1904 readers had the opportunity to delve into the magic of this book not only in Dutch but also in German, French and English.

Thanks to Count Bylandt's tome, readers of this book have the opportunity to learn exactly how the Lowchen was described in 1904, when it was called the 'Little Lion Dog.' This description follows:

General Appearance: A small ladies' dog, very active and intelligent, always one-third of the body

'La Dame et La Licorne' (The Lady and The Unicorn) is a fine 15th-century tapestry from France. The dog depicted is likely an ancestor of the Lowchen. This tapestry hangs in a museum in Paris.

to be clipped or shaved, giving him with his profuse collar the appearance of a lion in miniature.

Head: Short; skull rather broad.

Nose: Black; not turned up.

Eyes: Round, large and intelligent, dark in colour; eyelids dark.

Ears: Long and hanging, well feathered.

Body: Small, short but well proportioned.

Legs: Fine and straight.

Feet: Small and round; nails dark in colour.

Tail: Of medium length, clipped at the root and well feathered at the tip.

Coat: Rather long and wavy, but not curly.

Colour: All colours, self-coloured or parti-colours; the most preferable colours are the self-coloured white, black and lemon.

Height at shoulder: From 8 to 14 inches.

Weight: From 5 to 9 lbs.

For those who prefer to think in metric terms, the foreign

> **DID YOU KNOW?**
> Frequently one finds a lion on the tomb of a knight who was killed in battle, but it is often said that if a knight died a less valiant death, the depiction on his tomb was that of a Little Lion Dog.

language texts indicated 8 to 14 inches as the equivalent of 20 to 35 cms for the dog's height at shoulder, and 5 to 9 lbs as the equivalent of 2 to 4 kgs for the dog's weight.

'SAVIOURS' OF THE BREED

At the beginning of the twentieth century, there were few breeders of Lowchens. One of these was Mme de Connick of Diegheim and it was she, along with her husband Max, who is generally accepted as having kept the breed flag flying.

In the early twentieth century, the Lowchen was undoubtedly rare, and after the Second World War the breed is reputed to have been effectively 'saved from extinction' by a somewhat eccentric, elderly Belgian lady, Mme Bennert. Mme Bennert had originally owned a white bitch that she had bought from the Connicks, people who had already shown with success. After this, she was said to have scoured the streets of Brussels in search of Lowchens and she found two bitches that she considered typical specimens. One was blue and the other biscuit in colour. She also discovered a blue male, and with these three Lowchens she was able to begin a breeding programme. She also acquired a third bitch, and was to spend the next 20 years devoted to the breed and its improvement. Thanks to her careful breeding, all post-war Lowchens are believed to have been descended from Mrs Bennert's stock.

The first litter was whelped on 13 April 1948, but in those formative years dogs were often registered only with one name. Therefore, several Lowchens had to be bred before Mrs Bennert's affix 'de la Souveaine' could be added. So it is that many of the Lowchens that were bred by this staunch lady supporter of the breed are not immediately evident in early pedigrees.

Two breeders who founded their own kennels on Mrs

Once called the Little Lion Dog, the Lowchen is described as a small ladies' dog whose clip gives him the appearance of the lion.

Bennert's breeding were Mme de Meuleniere and Dr Hans Rickert, who effectively carried on Mme Bennert's work. All early Lowchens imported to the UK were dogs of Dr Rickert's breeding or were traced back to his stock.

THE LOWCHEN IN ART

Dogs that clearly resemble the Lowchen of today are to be found in fourteenth-century French tapestries. They also appear on German woodcuts and in Belgian

> **DID YOU KNOW?**
> Under the rules of the Fédération Cynologique Internationale, better known as the FCI, the breed was originally recognised under the name 'Le Petit Lion Chien Bichon.' This arose from dogs from Lyon in the south of France fitting this description.

paintings, so it seems clear that they were known over a wide geographical area of Europe.

The Lowchen was a favourite of Renaissance artists, and can be found in 'The Lady and the Unicorn' tapestries as well as in works by Albrecht Durer, particularly his woodcuts. In Durer's work, the Lowchen's personality clearly shines through, so these are not only representations of the breed's physical form. Goya was another artist who included the Lowchen in his paintings, such as in one of the Duchess of Alba (who apparently owned several such dogs) that was painted in 1795.

THE LOWCHEN IN BRITAIN

There is written material suggesting that the Lowchen was in Britain in the eighteenth century, but it was not known in modern-day Britain until 1968, when they were imported from Germany by Mrs Stenning and Mrs Banks. At that time there were only a few Lowchens known throughout the world and the imports were rather closely related. It was most fortunate that a particular bitch bred with apparent frequency seems not to have carried any hereditary faults; if she had, this may have spelled disaster for the breed. Indeed there was also very close breeding involved in other breeding programmes, so the Lowchen has been fortunate to remain a breed without any known major defects.

Two particularly important imports were Butzi vd Lowen and her son, Itzi, who arrived in Britain as a puppy. Subsequently mated together, they produced Cluneen Adam Adamant, who, in 1976, had the distinction of becoming the first champion in the breed both in Ireland and in the UK. Adam's dam, Butzi, also gained the title of Irish Champion.

The first set of Challenge Certificates for Lowchens in the UK was awarded at Crufts in 1976. The judge was the highly renowned Mrs Catherine Sutton, who awarded Prawls Meg Merilees, a double granddaughter of Adam Adamant, Best of Breed and Bitch CC. Adam took the very first Challenge Certificate in dogs at Crufts under the same judge. The first bitch to become a champion in the breed in Britain was Littlecourt Emma.

DID YOU KNOW?
In 1983 a 'Swedish Lowchen Circle' was established, and every year the club holds a show, which is judged by a specialist. There are now around 300 Lowchens in Sweden, a country that holds CC shows for the breed.

In the breed's early years in Britain there were 13 imports, and 10 of these were included in breeding programmes. Only three years later, the Lowchen found itself being exported out of Britain, going as far afield as the USA, Canada and Australia. Others went to European countries: Sweden, Finland, Holland and France. It took some years before the Lowchen Club was formed, which is still in existence and is the only club for the breed in Britain.

Competing in the show ring, the Lowchen is a naturally responsive and proud contestant. In the UK, the breed has had championship status since 1976.

GENUS *CANIS*

Dogs and wolves are members of the genus *Canis*. Wolves are known scientifically as *Canis lupus* while dogs are known as *Canis domesticus*. Dogs and wolves are known to interbreed. The term *canine* derives from the Latin derived word *Canis*. The term 'dog' has no scientific basis but has been used for thousands of years. The origin of the word 'dog' has never been authoritatively ascertained.

PUBLIC UNFAMILIARITY WITH THE BREED

In the early years of the Lowchen's history in Britain, breeders found it difficult to sell their puppies, as people simply did not know what they were. Few had ever even heard of a Lowchen. However, the American television programme *Hart to Hart* featured an unclipped Lowchen named 'Freeway,' and this played an instrumental part in bringing notice to this hitherto 'unknown' breed.

THE LOWCHEN IN THE USA

The breed was brought to the attention of the American public in 1970 when photos of two of Dr Rickert's Lowchens, described as 'living antiques,' appeared in a magazine. It was believed that there were then

The Lowchen with unclipped coat, not in the lion trim, hardly hints of its style when properly trimmed.

only 40 Lowchens alive and that Dr Rickert owned 10 of them!

The first member of the breed to arrive in the USA was from Britain. An announcement the Lowchen's arrival in the *New York Times* attracted Robert and Carole Yhlen to the breed, initially because both of them were born under the star sign of Leo. They soon acquired several Lowchens and became great devotees of the breed.

The first Lowchen to hold an obedience title in the USA was Charlie Brown, a charming dog who was something of a 'clown,' and a dog who attracted many people to the breed. Charlie used to carry a sign saying, 'Hi! My name is Charlie Brown and I'm a (smart) Little Lion Dog.' He would sit on a crate, holding this sign seemingly forever, his owners telling onlookers that he was so smart that he had written the sign himself and that writing was a skill that took Charlie

only two weeks to learn! Of course it was said 'tongue in cheek,' but it is an example of how clever Charlie was reputed to be.

In the USA a breed club was set up in 1972, and the Lowchen was approved for American Kennel Club registration and competition in 1995. On 1 April 1996 the breed entered the Miscellaneous Class. Since 1 January 1999 the Lowchen has been eligible to compete in the American Kennel Club's Non-Sporting Group.

Properly trimmed in the lion clip, the Lowchen is a distinctive pure-bred dog.

DID YOU KNOW?

Although it has been said that the Lowchen is a water dog, this is highly unlikely. While many Lowchens seem to enjoy water and have no fear of it, their coat is not one that would be effective as insulation when working in wet conditions.

Characteristics of the

LOWCHEN

WHY THE LOWCHEN?

The Lowchen is reasonably small in size, but has a great personality. He is fun to own and fun to look at, especially when clipped in his distinctive 'lion trim.' Indeed, many owners describe themselves as 'living with a pride of lions,' something both owners and 'lions' seem to thoroughly enjoy.

As a breed, Lowchens seem to be very happy with their lives and rarely have any objection to meeting both people and dogs, whatever their size! According to the breed standard, the Lowchen is not only cheerful, happy and lively but also intelligent and affectionate. This breed should certainly show no sign of aggression.

Some pet owners prefer to leave their Lowchens with long coats all over their bodies. However, the lion trim is one of the characteristics of the breed. In any case, a coat clipped into the lion trim is much easier to keep clean and is probably more comfortable for the dog. Alternatively, some pet owners like to keep their Lowchens in what is known as a 'puppy trim,' with the hair kept fairly short, the same length all over the body. So, whether caring for the coat in the lion trim, in keeping with centuries of tradition, in a natural state or in a puppy trim, the coat will need some looking after. Time must be dedicated to this aspect of canine care if selecting a Lowchen to share one's life; grooming to some extent should be carried out every day.

The Lowchen is a fairly long-lived breed and can often reach 15 years of age or more, another factor that must be seriously contemplated before deciding that this is really the breed for you. Clearly, when taking a new animal into your home, the ultimate aim will be that the dog remains with you for life.

The Lowchen has come through times when it clearly has not been as popular as might have been expected; indeed, in the past the breed has experienced times where it has been on the very brink of extinction. However, in recent decades the breed has risen rather rapidly in popularity, and on average there are now between 100 and 140 Lowchen puppies newly registered with The Kennel Club each year. Undoubtedly, the breed is now much better known; its many wonderful traits have caused it to become appreciated in many countries throughout the world.

PHYSICAL CHARACTERISTICS

The Lowchen is classified in Britain as a Toy breed, although it is not as small as some of the other Toys. The Lowchen stands some 22–33 cms (10–13 ins) high. Although strong and sturdy in bone, the Lowchen should never be coarse in any way. Indeed, the breed's size makes it eminently suitable for life in a town, although of course Lowchens can also thoroughly enjoy a more rural life when given the opportunity. This is an active and well-balanced breed, and, with its tail carried gaily on the move and its head held proudly and high, the Lowchen is undoubtedly a dog with great style.

DID YOU KNOW?

In the 1970s, the late Harry Glover described the Lowchen as having a quite delightful temperament. He said that Lowchens were friendly with everyone and became very attached to their owners. Mr Glover considered them lively and boisterous, but kind and playful with no vices, making the Lowchen an admirable house pet and friend of the family.

SKIN PROBLEMS

Eczema and dermatitis are skin problems that occur in many breeds and they can often be a tricky problem to solve. Frequent bathing of the dog will remove skin oils and will cause the problem to worsen. Allergies to food or something in the environment can also cause the problem. Consider trying homeopathic remedies in addition to seeing your vet for direction.

COLOUR AND COAT

Any coat colour or combination of colours is acceptable in the Lowchen; it is the only breed within the Bichon 'family' that can be of any colour. As no preference is given, the breed can be seen in a variety of eye-catching hues and a line-up of Lowchens seen in the show ring can be a veritable feast for the eyes. Coat colour can change between puppyhood and adulthood, but there seems to be a much wider variation of colour in the breed now than there was in days gone by. Of course, some people will have their own personal colour preferences, but what is of utmost importance is the dog's soundness of mentality and structure, not the colour of its coat!

The breed is always exhibited in the show ring in 'lion trim,' and that is the way most people like to keep a Lowchen's coat, whether or not it is a show dog. The untrimmed part of the coat is fairly long and, though wavy, should never be curly. In America the coat is described as 'rather dense and moderately soft in texture' and it is quite clearly stated that the untrimmed area of the coat should not be 'smoothed, shortened, shaped or otherwise tidied with anything other than a comb or brush.' Wiry, woolly, curly and flat coats are untypical of this breed.

The coat on the clipped tail of the Lowchen is another distinctive feature, clipped as it is from its base to about half its length, leaving a plume at the end of the tail. The feet, too, are clipped, as are the legs, just leaving bracelets of hair on all four legs.

Before closing this short section concerning coat, it is worth mentioning that, very occasionally, short-coated specimens of the breed are born. These are throwbacks to one of the first bitches imported to Britain, who was herself short-coated. Varying coat patterns can occur in these short-coated dogs, but usually the coat is thick and stands out from the body; this is quite different from that of a typically coated Lowchen. On face and legs the coat is generally shorter and lies flat. Such unusual coat patterns, if they occur, can usually be noticed by the time a puppy is between six and eight weeks of age. This means that before a puppy leaves for its new home, a breeder should have some indication about whether the coat will be typical or not. It must be stressed, though, that short-coated Lowchens are found only rarely.

DID YOU KNOW?
The easiest method of weighing your Lowchen is on the bathroom scales. First weigh yourself alone, then a second time while holding the dog in your arms. Deduct one from the other to obtain the accurate weight of your dog.

PERSONALITY
With its alert, outgoing, affectionate and inquisitive personality, the Lowchen makes a delightful pet and is not as hyperactive as some breeds. Friendly by nature, it is said that Lowchens alternate between impishness and innocence, a rather quaint, yet apt, description.

Lowchens seem able to out-think their owners, apparently having the answers sorted out in their little heads well before their human counterparts. When something of which you disapprove has happened, they also have a curious way of looking at you with their melting eyes as if to say, 'It wasn't me.' Most Lowchens are also perfectly capable of turning a 'deaf ear' when it suits them to do so.

The nature of the Lowchen is happy and outgoing, winning the breed numerous friends whether or not they are owners of Lowchens themselves. Many Lowchens are described as 'clowns,' and all are ready to charm their way into people's hearts. However, it is important that Lowchens are socialised, for, as with other breeds, there is always the danger that they may become withdrawn if they do not come into contact with people regularly.

Usually Lowchens are admirably suited to family life and get on well with all members of the household. As they do not shed their coats, Lowchens often make good pet for families in which there are sufferers of asthma.

What the Lowchen Enjoys

Lowchens are agile, alert and intelligent dogs. This, coupled with their sturdy well-knit frames,

DOGS, DOGS, GOOD FOR YOUR HEART!
People usually purchase dogs for companionship, but studies show that dogs can help to improve their owners' health and level of activity, as well as lower a human's risk of coronary heart disease. Without even realising it, when a person puts time into exercising, grooming and feeding a dog, he also puts more time into his own personal health care. Dog owners establish a more routine schedule for their dogs to follow, which can have positive effects on a human's health. Dogs also teach us patience, offer unconditional love and provide the joy of having a furry friend to pet!

makes them suitable candidates both for obedience and agility activities. Indeed, some are highly successful in these areas. Also, because they can spring up so easily on their back legs, some Lowchens even take part in Flyball competition. So adaptable is this charming little breed that some Lowchens work as hearing dogs for the deaf, a challenging and admirable employ that must undoubtedly be greatly appreciated by their owners.

Something else enjoyed by the occasional Lowchen is the 'art of escapology,' which can present obvious problems. Some have been known to scale six-foot fences, and it has not been unknown for the odd Lowchen to escape from a crate by means of carefully dismantling the interior springs that hold the door closed. Owners should be alert to all possibilities!

The Lowchen meets the Griffon Bruxellois. Lowchens get on well with other well-behaved pets. They are neither quarrelsome nor aggressive with other dogs.

DID YOU KNOW?
Elderly Lowchens can be prone to putting on excess weight, and this is more likely if a bitch has been spayed. Over-eating, or feeding the wrong foods or too many titbits may well be the cause. Often an older dog requires a slightly different diet from a younger one.

LOWCHENS AND CHILDREN

Provided that parents have trained their children to treat dogs gently, being neither rough nor aggressive, most Lowchens thoroughly enjoy playing with youngsters. It must, though, be understood that young children should always be supervised when in the company of dogs so that accidents do not happen, however unintentional they might be.

LOWCHENS AND OTHER FAMILY PETS

When one animal is introduced to another, careful supervision is always essential. Most Lowchens are quite prepared to associate with other animals, but much understandably depends on the personality of the other animal. Some older dogs or cats may not take readily to newcomers to the household, although others accept them well. When a Lowchen does find another canine or feline friend, usually the relationship is lasting and sincere.

Some Lowchens share their family homes with other dogs that are much larger, and this usually appears to result in thoroughly happy relationships. Many Lowchen owners say that their dogs simply do not realise that they are meant to be pampered Toy dogs; instead, they like to join in the lifestyles and activities of much larger canine friends.

An obedience-trained dog in the USA took readily to penning domesticated goats with apparently no effort at all. He had carefully watched his friend, the family Border Collie, doing the same and thought he would follow his example—with admirable results!

HEALTH CONSIDERATIONS

In general, the Lowchen is a healthy, hardy little dog that rarely suffers from health problems. However, as in so many

TAKING CARE

Science is showing that as people take care of their pets, the pets are taking care of their owners. A study in 1998, published in the *American Journal of Cardiology,* found that having a pet can prolong his owner's life. Pet owners have lower blood pressure, and pets help their owners to relax and keep them more physically fit. It was also found that pets help to keep the elderly connected to their community.

The eyes of the Lowchen can be sensitive due to their size and the amount of hair that surrounds them. Pet dogs should have the hair around their eyes trimmed, though this is not acceptable for show dogs.

other breeds, certain heath problems can arise. If owners are aware of the problems that can occur, they are undoubtedly in a position to deal with them in the best manner possible. Some problems are genetic and are carried via heredity, but others are not.

PATELLAR LUXATION

Lowchens, like many other toy breeds, occasionally suffer from trouble with the knee joints, known as patellar luxation. It is important that dogs thus affected should not be overweight, for this is likely to exacerbate the problem. Many dogs with patellar luxation live with the problem without experiencing pain, but surgery sometimes has to be considered.

BLADDER STONES

Although found infrequently, bladder stones can sometimes cause a problem, as they are found more often in small breeds than in larger ones. Symptoms include frequent passing of urine, blood in the urine, straining to pass water, general weakness, depression and loss of appetite.

Urgent veterinary attention is necessary, for stones in the bladder can lead to irreparable kidney damage and death can eventually result. In many cases stones can be dissolved by a special diet under veterinary supervision, but certain types require surgical removal.

TEETH

It is important to pay close attention to the care of teeth and gums so that they remain as healthy as possible throughout a Lowchen's long life. Stringent tooth care helps prevent decay, infection and resultant loss of teeth.

DO YOU WANT TO LIVE LONGER?
If you like to volunteer, it is wonderful if you can take your dog to a nursing home once a week for several hours. The elder community loves to have a dog to visit with and often your dog will bring a bit of companionship to someone who is lonely or somewhat detached from the world. You will be not only bringing happiness to someone else but keeping your little dog busy—and we haven't even mentioned the fact that it has been discovered that volunteering helps to increase your own longevity!

CORRECTIVE SURGERY
Surgery is often used to correct genetic bone diseases in dogs. Usually the problems present themselves early in the dog's life and must be treated before bone growth stops.

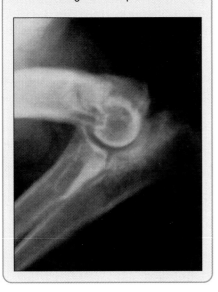

Infection in the gums may not just stop there. The bacteria from a gum infection is carried through the bloodstream, the result of which can be liver, kidney, heart and joint disease. This is all the more reason to appreciate that regular dental care is always of the utmost importance.

EYES

In some countries, but not in Britain, Lowchen owners trim the hair around the eyes to make the eyes look bigger. This, in consequence, prevents any possibility of hair irritating the eyes. Tear staining below the eyes, something more easily noticed on white and light-coloured dogs, can sometimes be found, but this can usually be eased with mild eye drops.

Clearly it is necessary to pay attention to keeping the eyes clean; this should be a routine aspect of grooming the Lowchen.

Ears

Because the Lowchen's ears hang close to the head and have long fringing in accordance with the breed standard, there can be lack of ventilation. It is therefore important that the ears are checked regularly and that excess hair is carefully plucked from inside the ear to avoid infection.

Signs of an infected ear include a brown, odorous discharge that leads to the ear's becoming red, inflamed and sore. At this stage, the dog will scratch at the ear and may hold his head on one side because of the pain.

Bad Breath

Offensive breath is usually the result of problems with teeth and gums, but it can also be caused by indigestion or may sometimes be related to the kidneys.

In cases of digestive problems giving rise to bad breath, charcoal, either in the form of tablets or granules, can often help. A useful aid to masking bad breath is the use of chlorophyll tablets.

Licking

Sometimes even a minor irritation will cause a dog to lick at its own skin, and this can all too easily develop into a habit. Licking is likely to make the coat turn pink in colour, so this must be prevented. Sometimes licking can be associated with boredom; therefore, owners should be sure their Lowchens have plenty with which to entertain and occupy themselves at all times! Several good preparations are now available to dissuade a dog from licking; usually they taste rather bitter, and the habit can frequently be stopped by use of such an agent.

Other Health Problems

It must be understood that there are many other health problems that can occur in dogs, but it is not possible to outline them all here. As you get to know your Lowchen, you will also come to recognise if ever he is 'off colour,' at which time a quick trip to the vet can often help to 'nip a problem in the bud' so that suitable care and any necessary medication may be given as early as possible.

Because of their small size, Lowchens are popular with children and many children exhibit their dogs at local dog shows.

The Kennel Club breed standard for the Lowchen is effectively a 'blueprint' for the breed. It sets down the various points of the dog in words, enabling a visual picture to be conjured up in the mind of the reader. However, this is more easily said than done. Not only do standards vary from country to country, but people's interpretations of breed standards vary also. It is this difference of interpretation that makes judges select different dogs for top honours, for their opinions differ as to which dog most closely fits the breed standard. That is not to say that a good dog does not win regularly under different judges, nor that an inferior dog may rarely even be placed at a show, at least not among quality competition.

The breed standard given here is that authorised by the English Kennel Club. It is relatively short compared with the standards of many other breeds, so a little further explanation is probably helpful. As with most breeds, there are variances between the standard used in Britain and that used in the USA, and indeed the American standard for the breed goes into considerably more detail and is therefore more comprehensive.

The height of the Lowchen in the USA is a little larger, with a specified ideal height of 12 to 14 inches at withers (30.5–35.5 cms), and although a short loin is called for, the body is described as 'just off square.' Another significant difference is that in Britain a moderate tuck-up is required, whereas in America the descriptive word used for the tuck-up is 'slight.'

The English standard makes no mention of the positioning of the eyes, but the American Kennel Club's (AKC's) standard says they should be 'set well apart and forward looking.' Regarding feet, again there is quite a difference between the two standards. In Britain it is indicated that they only need to be small and round, but the American standard goes into much more detail, which is worthy of quotation for our readers' reference.

'The forefeet point straight ahead, and are well arched with deep pads and the two center toes are slightly in advance of the two outer toes. The nails are relatively short. A tight foot is preferred, and a splayed foot is to be penalised. ... The hindfeet are

slightly smaller than the forefeet, and are well arched with deep pads.'

Having examined these differences, let us now study the English Kennel Club's breed standard.

THE KENNEL CLUB STANDARD FOR THE LOWCHEN

General Appearance: Coat clipped in traditional lion clip, tail also clipped, topped with plume, giving appearance of a little lion. Strongly built, active, well balanced and alert.

Characteristics: Gay, happy, lively little dog.

Temperament: Intelligent, affectionate, showing no sign of aggression.

Head and Skull: Short, fairly broad. Skull flat between the ears, head carried proud and high. Well defined stop; short, strong muzzle.

Eyes: Round, dark, large and intelligent. Unbroken pigmentation of eye rims, pigment to be in accordance with coat colour.

Ears: Ears pendant, of moderate length with long fringing.

Mouth: Jaws strong, with perfect, regular and complete scissor bite, i.e. upper teeth closely overlapping lower teeth and set square to the jaws.

Neck: Good length, proudly arched.

Forequarters: Forelegs straight and fine. Shoulders well laid.

Round eyes and a short, flat skull between the ears are important characteristics of the Lowchen.

A Lowchen with the traditional lion clip.

THE IDEAL SPECIMEN

According to The Kennel Club, 'The Breed Standard is the "Blueprint" of the ideal specimen in each breed approved by a governing body, e.g. The Kennel Club, the Fédération Cynologique International (FCI) and the American Kennel Club.

'The Kennel Club writes and revises Breed Standards taking account of the advice of Breed Councils/Clubs. Breed Standards are not changed lightly to avoid "changing the standard to fit the current dogs" and the health and well-being of future dogs is always taken into account when new standards are prepared or existing ones altered.'

Body: Short, strong and well proportioned. Level topline. Ribs well sprung. Strong loin with moderate tuck-up.

Hindquarters: Hindlegs well muscled, with good turn of stifle; straight when viewed from rear.

Feet: Small, round.

Tail: Medium length, clipped with tuft of hair to resemble a plume. Carried gaily on move.

Gait/Movement: Free, parallel movement fore and aft, no hackneyed action.

Coat: Fairly long, wavy, never curly. Single coat of soft texture.

Colour: Any colour or combination of colours permissible.

Size: Height at withers 25–33 cms (10–13 ins).

Faults: Any departure from the foregoing points should be considered a fault and the seriousness with which the fault should be regarded should be in exact proportion to its degree.

Note: Male animals should have two apparently normal testicles fully descended into the scrotum.

Although a great deal can be learned from the breed standard,

In order to improve the breed with each new generation, Lowchen breeders select their stock with an eye on the breed standard and the other eye on good luck.

only by seeing good-quality, typical specimens can one really learn to appreciate the breed's merits. Therefore, readers interested in showing their Lowchens should watch other dogs being exhibited and should learn as much as possible from established breeders and exhibitors.

It is sensible to attend any specialist breed seminars that may be hosted by breed clubs. Here the finer points of the breed can be explained fully and discussed. There is usually a dog, or perhaps several, available for demonstration purposes, and there may even be an opportunity for participants to feel beneath the coat for the structure of the animal.

Just a few elaborations on the breed standard are, however, worthy of brief comment here.

One of the first points of the Lowchen mentioned in the standard is the head, and this is an extremely important aspect of the breed. The head should neither be coarse nor weak, and although the breed standard calls for a 'short' muzzle, it should not be too short or typicality of expression will be lost. The breed standard also requires the muzzle to be strong, so there should be no distinct tapering of the muzzle toward the end. The correct muzzle shape will allow the teeth to be set fairly squarely into the jaw. The stop, which is the indentation between the eyes where the nasal bone and skull meet, is to be well defined, though not so exaggerated as in a very short-nosed breed like the Shih Tzu. If there were insufficient stop, the desired facial expression of the Lowchen would certainly not be achieved.

The skull is flat between the ears, with the ears being well fringed and framing the head. Eyes should be round, large and dark, and it is a requirement in the breed standard that the pigment surrounding the eyes is unbroken. This means that the pigment should not be broken up with a lighter colour, although pigment may vary slightly in accordance with coat colour.

The British breed standard gives little explanation concerning colour, but it is generally accepted in the breed that, because the Lowchen is found in any colour or combination of colours, nose pigment should certainly be dark, but black or brown according to the colour of the coat.

Although the neck should be proudly arched, it should not be swan-like. This is a trait that seems to be 'accepted' by enthusiasts in many breeds, but which is not necessarily the result of soundly constructed forequarters. The shoulders are to be well laid, leading in to a nice level topline, which should be held firmly when the dog is on the move.

Leg length on the Lowchen is important. If overall leg length is too short, the dog will not be well-balanced, in keeping with the standard. Moreover, if the bone in the upper arm is too short, not only may the overall leg length be too short but the dog also will most probably move with a hackneyed action, lifting the front feet high. A hackneyed action is a type of movement clearly unwanted in the breed. The way the dog moves in front is, however, decided to a large extent by hind construction as well. If, for example, the hindquarters are better angulated than the forequarters, the dog will have to compensate in some way. The Lowchen should have a good turn of stifle and the hindlegs are to be well muscled, allowing plenty of drive from the rear. The Lowchen should be able to move freely, with parallel movement, both front and rear, and there should be a good length of stride.

Something not actually mentioned in the breed standard is a Lowchen's bottom, which personally I find rather a pity, as everyone who understands the breed loves to see a Lowchen with a lovely round bottom. This is created by the pelvic structure beneath being fairly wide and covered with both flesh and muscle. The hind legs should also be well muscled, though no aspect of musculature on this breed should be over-exaggerated as is sometimes required in a few much larger breeds. On the other hand, very narrow, pinched hindquarters are quite untypical of this strongly built, sturdy little breed.

Regarding the dog's general appearance, the coat is a major contributing factor. It is clearly stated in the opening paragraph of the breed standard that the coat is to be clipped in the traditional lion trim.

In conclusion, the Lowchen is a most attractive little dog in every way and, despite a relatively small gene pool, breeders have gone a long way in stabilising the overall sound and typical construction of this healthy breed. Indeed it is now, as it was in centuries past, a well-deserved favourite among members of the dog-loving fraternity.

The Lowchen's gait (or movement) is evaluated by the judge in the show ring. According to the breed standard, gait must be free with parallel movement fore and aft.

You have probably decided on a Lowchen as your choice of pet following a visit to the home of a friend or acquaintance, where you saw an enchanting Lowchen,

PUPPY SELECTION

Your selection of a good puppy can be determined by your needs. A show potential or a good pet? It is your choice. Every puppy, however, should be of good temperament. Although show-quality puppies are bred and raised with emphasis on physical conformation, responsible breeders strive for equally good temperament. Do not buy from a breeder who concentrates solely on physical beauty at the expense of personality.

looking clean and tidy in his lion clip, wandering confidently around the house and joining politely in the family fun. However, as a new owner you must realise that a good deal of care, commitment and careful training goes into raising a boisterous puppy so that your pet turns into a well-behaved adult. In deciding to take on a new puppy you will be committing yourself to approximately 15 years of responsibility. No dog should be discarded after a few months, or even a few years, after the novelty has worn off. Instead, your Lowchen should be joining your household to spend the rest of its days with you.

Although temperamentally a Lowchen is much easier to look after than many other breeds, you will still need to carry out a certain amount of training. Unlike some of the larger, guarding breeds, it will not respond well to overly strict training. Instead, you will need to take a firm but gentle approach in order to get the very best out of your pet.

A Lowchen generally likes to be clean around the house, but you will need to teach your puppy what is and what is not expected. You will need to be consistent in your instructions; it is no good accepting certain behaviour one day and not the next. Not only will your puppy simply not understand, he will be utterly confused. Your Lowchen will want to please you, so you will need to demonstrate clearly how your puppy is to achieve this.

Although the dog you are taking into your home will be small, and therefore probably less troublesome than a large dog, there will undoubtedly be a period of settling in. This will be great fun, but you must be prepared for mishaps around the home during the first few weeks of your life together. It will be important that precious ornaments are kept well out of harm's way, and you will have to think twice about where you place hot cups of coffee or anything breakable. Accidents can and do happen, so you will need to think ahead in an effort to avoid these. Electric cables must be carefully concealed, and your puppy must be taught where he is allowed to go and which areas are 'off-limits.'

Before making a commitment to a new puppy, do also think carefully about your future holiday plans. Depending on the country in which you live, your dog may or may not be able to travel abroad with you. Because of

PREPARING FOR PUP

Unfortunately, when a puppy is bought by someone who does not take into consideration the time and attention that dog ownership requires, it is the puppy who suffers when he is either abandoned or placed in a shelter by a frustrated owner. So all of the 'homework' you do in preparation for your pup's arrival will benefit you both. The more informed you are, the more you will know what to expect and the better equipped you will be to handle the ups and downs of raising a puppy. Hopefully, everyone in the household is willing to do his part in raising and caring for the pup. The anticipation of owning a dog often brings a lot of promises from excited family members: 'I will walk him every day,' 'I will feed him,' 'I will housebreak him,' etc., but these things take time and effort, and promises can easily be forgotten once the novelty of the new pet has worn off.

PUPPY APPEARANCE

Your puppy should have a well-fed appearance but not a distended abdomen, which may indicate worms or incorrect feeding, or both. The body should be firm, with a solid feel. The skin of the abdomen should be pale pink and clean, without signs of scratching or rash. Check the hind legs to make certain that dewclaws were removed, if any were present at birth.

DID YOU KNOW?

You should not even think about buying a puppy that looks sick, undernourished, overly frightened or nervous. Sometimes a timid puppy will warm up to you after a 30-minute 'let's-get-acquainted' session.

quarantine laws, no dog can travel freely in and out of Britain, so this must be carefully considered ahead of your purchase. If you have thought things through carefully and discussed the matter thoroughly with all of the members of your family, you should have come to the right decision. If you decide that a Lowchen should join your family, this will hopefully be a happy, long-term relationship for all parties concerned.

BUYING A LOWCHEN PUPPY

Although you may be looking for a Lowchen as a pet rather than as a show dog, this does not mean that you want a dog that is in any way 'second-rate.' A caring breeder will have brought up the entire litter of puppies with the same amount of dedication, and a puppy destined for a pet home should be just as healthy as one that hopes to end up in the show ring.

Because you have carefully selected this breed, you will want a Lowchen that is a typical specimen, both in looks and in temperament. In your endeavours to find such a puppy you will have to select the breeder with care. The English Kennel Club (or the national kennel club of the country in which you live) will almost certainly be able to give you names of the secretaries of any club for the breed, or perhaps a contact within a club that caters to a number of breeds, among which is the Lowchen. These people can possibly put you in touch with breeders who may have puppies for sale. However, although they can point you in the right direction, it will be up to you to do your homework carefully, and you may well find that your name has to take its

INSURANCE

Many good breeders will offer you insurance with your new puppy, which is an excellent idea. The first few weeks of insurance will probably be covered free of charge or with only minimal cost, allowing you to take up the policy when this expires. If you own a pet dog, it is sensible to take out such a policy as veterinary fees can be high, although routine vaccinations and boosters are not covered. Look carefully at the many options open to you before deciding which suits you best.

BOY OR GIRL?

An important consideration to be discussed is the sex of your puppy. For a family companion, a bitch may be the better choice, considering the female's inbred concern for all young creatures and her accompanying tolerance and patience. It is always advisable to spay a pet bitch, which may guarantee her a longer life.

DOCUMENTATION

Two important documents you will get from the breeder are the pup's pedigree and registration certificate. The breeder should register the litter and each pup with The Kennel Club, and it is necessary for you to have the paperwork if you plan on showing or breeding in the future.

Make sure you know the breeder's intentions on which type of registration he will obtain for the pup. There are limited registrations which may prohibit the dog from being shown, bred or from competing in non-conformation trials such as Working or Agility if the breeder feels that the pup is not of sufficient quality to do so. There is also a type of registration that will permit the dog in non-conformation competition only.

On the reverse side of the registration certificate, the new owner can find the transfer section which must be signed by the breeder.

When buying a puppy, it is wise to meet the dam as well. The puppies will inherit not only the mother's appearance but also her temperament.

some idea about which breeders appear to take most care of their stock and which are likely to have given their puppies the best possible start in life.

Clearly when selecting a puppy, the one you choose must be in good condition. The coat should look healthy and there should be no discharge from the eyes or nose. Ears should also be clean, and of course there should be absolutely no sign of parasites; likewise, there should be no evidence of parasites or rashes on the skin. It goes without saying that the puppy you choose should

place on a waiting list.

Even though you are probably not looking for a show dog, it is always a good idea to visit a show so that you can see quality specimens of the breed. This will also give you an opportunity to meet breeders who will probably be able to answer some of your queries. In addition, you will get

not have evidence of loose
motions. Always check the bite of
your selected puppy to be sure
that it is neither overshot nor
undershot.

When buying your puppy, you
will need to know about vaccinations, those already given and
those still due. It is important that
any injections already given by a
veterinary surgeon are properly
documented. A worming routine
is also vital for any young puppy;
the breeder should be able to tell
you exactly what treatment has
been given, when it has been
administered and how you should
continue.

When you visit the litter,
always insist that you see the
puppy's dam and, if possible, the
sire. However, frequently the sire
will not be owned by the breeder,
but a photograph may be available
for you to see. Ask if the breeder
has any other of the puppy's
relations that you could meet. For
example, there may be an older
half-sister or half-brother, and it
would be interesting for you to
see how they have turned out as
far as eventual size, coat quality,
temperament and so on.

Be certain, too, if you decide
to buy a puppy, that all relevant
documentation is provided at the
time of sale. You will need a copy
of the pedigree, preferably Kennel
Club registration documents,
vaccination certificates and a
feeding chart so that you know

DID YOU KNOW?
Breeders rarely release Lowchen
puppies until they are around 12
weeks, given their petite sizes. If
a breeder has a puppy that is 12
weeks or more, it is likely well
socialised and housetrained. Be
sure that it is otherwise healthy
before deciding to take it home.

exactly how the puppy has been
fed and how you should continue.
Some careful breeders provide
their puppy buyers with a small
amount of food. This prevents the
risk of an upset tummy, allowing
for a gradual change of diet if that
particular brand of food is not
locally available.

WHERE TO BEGIN?
If you are convinced that the
Lowchen is the ideal dog for you,

it's time to begin your search. Locating a litter of Lowchens will require a bit of research. You should enquire about breeders who enjoy a good reputation in the breed. You are looking for an established breeder with outstanding dog ethics and a strong commitment to the breed. New owners should have as many questions as they have doubts. An established breeder is indeed the one to answer your four million questions and make you comfortable with your choice of the Lowchen. An established breeder will sell you a puppy at a fair price if, and only if, the breeder determines that you are a suitable, worthy owner of his dogs. An established breeder can be relied upon for advice, no matter what time of day or night. A reputable breeder will accept a puppy back, without questions, should you decide that this is not the right dog for you.

When choosing a breeder, reputation is much more important than convenience of location. Do not be overly impressed by breeders who run brag advertisements in the presses about their stupendous

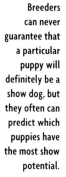

Breeders can never guarantee that a particular puppy will definitely be a show dog, but they often can predict which puppies have the most show potential.

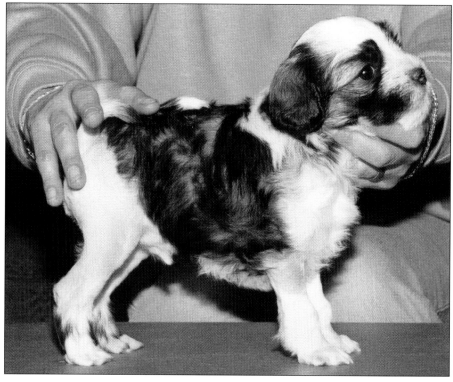

YOUR SCHEDULE...
If you lead an erratic, unpredictable life, with daily or weekly changes in your work requirements, consider the problems of owning a puppy. The new puppy has to be fed regularly, socialised (loved, petted, handled, introduced to other people) and, most importantly, allowed to visit outdoors for toilet training. As the dog gets older, it can be more tolerant of deviations in its feeding and toilet relief.

champions. The real quality breeders are quiet and unassuming. You hear about them at dog shows, by word of mouth. Choosing a breeder is an important first step in dog ownership. Fortunately, the majority of Lowchen breeders is devoted to the breed and its well being. New owners should have little problem finding a reputable breeder who doesn't live on the other side of the country (or in a different country).

Once you have contacted and met a breeder or two and made your choice about which breeder is best suited to your needs, it's time to visit the litter. Keep in mind that many top breeders have waiting lists. Sometimes new owners have to wait as long as two years for a puppy. If you are really committed to the breeder

whom you've selected, then you will wait (and hope for an early arrival!). If not, you may have to resort to your second or third choice breeder. Don't be too anxious, however. If the breeder doesn't have a waiting list, or any customers, there is probably a good reason. It's no different than visiting a pub with no clientele. The better pubs and restaurants always have a waiting list—and it's usually worth the wait. Besides, isn't a puppy more important than a pint?

Breeders commonly allow visitors to see the litter by around the fifth or sixth week, and puppies leave for their new homes between the eighth and tenth week. Breeders who permit their puppies to leave early are more interested in your pounds than their puppies' well-being. Puppies need to learn the rules of the pack from their dams, and

INHERIT THE MIND
In order to know whether or not a puppy will fit into your lifestyle, you need to assess his personality. A good way to do this is to interact with his parents. Your pup inherits not only his appearance but also his personality and temperament from the sire and dam. If the parents are fearful or overly aggressive, these same traits may likely show up in your puppy.

most dams continue teaching the pups manners and dos and don'ts until around the eighth week. Breeders spend significant amounts of time with the Lowchen toddlers so that they are able to interact with the 'other species,' i.e. humans.

PUPPY PERSONALITY
When a litter becomes available to you, choosing a pup out of all those adorable faces will not be an easy task! Sound temperament is of utmost importance, but each pup has its own personality and some may be better suited to you than others. A feisty, independent pup will do well in a home with older children and adults, while quiet, shy puppies will thrive in a home with minimum noise and distractions. Your breeder knows the pups best and should be able to guide you in the right direction.

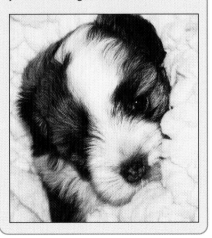

ARE YOU A FIT OWNER?
If the breeder from whom you are buying a puppy asks you a lot of personal questions, do not be insulted. Such a breeder wants to be sure that you will be a fit provider for his puppy.

Given the long history that dogs and humans have, bonding between the two species is natural but must be nurtured. A well-bred, well-socialised Lowchen pup wants nothing more than to be near you and please you.

COMMITMENT OF OWNERSHIP
Researching your breed, selecting a responsible breeder and observing as many pups as possible are all important steps on the way to dog ownership. It may seem like a lot of effort…and you have not even taken the pup home yet! Remember, though, you cannot be too careful when it comes to deciding on the type of dog you want and finding out about your prospective pup's background. Buying a puppy is not—or should not be—just another whimsical purchase. This is one instance in which you actually do get to choose your own family! You may be thinking that buying a puppy should be fun—it should not be so serious and so much work. Keep in mind

that your puppy is not a cuddly stuffed toy or decorative lawn ornament, but a creature that will become a real member of your family. You will come to realise that, while buying a puppy is a pleasurable and exciting endeavour, it is not something to be taken lightly. Relax...the fun will start when the pup comes home!

Always keep in mind that a puppy is nothing more than a baby in a furry disguise...a baby who is virtually helpless in a human world and who trusts his owner for fulfilment of his basic needs for survival. In addition to water and shelter, your pup needs care, protection, guidance and love. If you are not prepared to commit to this, then you are not prepared to own a dog.

Wait a minute, you say. How hard could this be? All of my neighbours own dogs and they seem to be doing just fine. Why should I have to worry about all of this? Well, you should not worry about it; in fact, you will probably find that once your Lowchen pup gets used to his new home, he will fall into his place in the family quite naturally. But it never hurts to emphasise the commitment of dog ownership. With some time and patience, it is really not too difficult to raise a curious and exuberant Lowchen pup to be a well-adjusted and well-mannered

'YOU BETTER SHOP AROUND!'
Finding a reputable breeder that sells healthy pups is very important, but make sure that the breeder you choose is not only someone you respect but also with whom you feel comfortable. Your breeder will be a resource long after you buy your puppy, and you must be able to call with reasonable questions without being made to feel like a pest! If you don't connect on a personal level, investigate some other breeders before making a final decision.

adult dog—a dog that could be your most loyal friend.

PREPARING PUPPY'S PLACE IN YOUR HOME
Researching your breed and finding a breeder are only two aspects of the 'homework' you will have to do before taking your

QUALITY FOOD
All dogs need a good quality food with an adequate supply of protein to develop their bones and muscles properly. Most dogs are not picky eaters but unless fed properly they can quickly succumb to skin problems.

Lowchen puppy home. You will also have to prepare your home and family for the new addition. Much as you would prepare a nursery for a newborn baby, you will need to designate a place in your home that will be the puppy's own. How you prepare your home will depend on how much freedom the dog will be allowed. Whatever you decide, you must ensure that he has a place that he can 'call his own.'

When you bring your new puppy into your home, you are bringing him into what will become his home as well. Obviously, you did not buy a puppy so that he could take over your house, but in order for a puppy to grow into a stable, well-adjusted dog, he has to feel comfortable in his surroundings. Remember, he is leaving the warmth and security of his mother and littermates, as well as the familiarity of the only place he has ever known, so it is important to make his transition as easy as possible. By preparing a place in your home for the puppy, you are making him feel as welcome as possible in a strange new place. It should not take him long to get used to it, but the sudden shock of being transplanted is somewhat traumatic for a young pup. Imagine how a small child would feel in the same situation—that is how your puppy must be feeling. It is up to you to reassure him and to let him know, 'Little chap, you are going to like it here!'

WHAT YOU SHOULD BUY

CRATE
To someone unfamiliar with the use of crates in dog training, it may seem like punishment to shut

a dog in a crate, but this is not the case at all. Although all breeders do not advocate crate training, more and more breeders and trainers are recommending crates as preferred tools for show puppies as well as pet puppies. Crates are not cruel—crates have many humane and highly effective uses in dog care and training. For example, crate training is a very popular and very successful toilet training method. A crate can keep your dog safe during travel and, perhaps most importantly, a crate provides your dog with a place of his own in your home. It serves as a 'doggie bedroom' of sorts—your Lowchen can curl up in his crate when he wants to sleep or when he just needs a break. Many dogs sleep in their crates overnight. With soft bedding and his favourite toy, a crate becomes a cosy pseudo-den for your dog. Like his ancestors, he too will seek out the comfort and retreat of a den—you just happen to be providing him with something a little more luxurious than what his early ancestors enjoyed.

As far as purchasing a crate, the type that you buy is up to you. It will most likely be one of the two most popular types: wire or fibreglass. There are advantages and disadvantages to each type. For example, a wire crate is more open, allowing the air to flow through and affording the dog a

PHOTO COURTESY OF DOSKOCIL.

view of what is going on around him while a fibreglass crate is sturdier. Both can double as travel crates, providing protection for the dog. The size of the crate is another thing to consider; you should purchase a crate that will accommodate your dog both as a pup and at full size. A small- to medium-sized crate will suffice

Your local pet shop will probably have a wide variety of crates from which you may choose the one which best suits your needs.

CRATE TRAINING TIPS

During crate training, you should partition off the section of the crate in which the pup stays. If he is given too big an area, this will hinder your training efforts. Crate training is based on the fact that a dog does not like to soil his sleeping quarters, so it is ineffective to keep a pup in a crate that is so big that he can eliminate in one end and get far enough away from it to sleep. Also, you want to make the crate den-like for the pup. Blankets and a favourite toy will make the crate cosy for the small pup; as he grows, you may want to evict some of his 'roommates' to make more room.

It will take some coaxing at first, but be patient. Given some time to get used to it, your pup will adapt to his new home-within-a-home quite nicely.

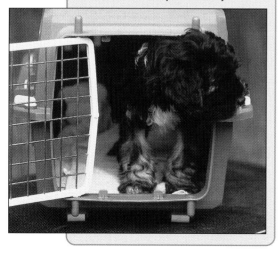

for a full-grown Lowchen, who stands between 10–13 inches high.

BEDDING

Veterinary bedding in the dog's crate will help the dog feel more at home and you may also like to pop in a small blanket. This will take the place of the leaves, twigs, etc., that the pup would use in the wild to make a den; the pup can make his own 'burrow' in the crate. Although your pup is far removed from his den-making ancestors, the denning instinct is still a part of his genetic makeup. Second, until you take your pup home, he has been sleeping amidst the warmth of his mother and littermates, and while a blanket is not the same as a warm, breathing body, it still provides heat and something with which to snuggle. You will want to wash your pup's bedding frequently in case he has an accident in his crate, and replace or remove any blanket that becomes ragged and starts to fall apart.

TOYS

Toys are a must for dogs of all ages, especially for curious playful pups. Puppies are the 'children' of the dog world, and what child does not love toys? Chew toys provide enjoyment for both dog and owner—your dog will enjoy playing with his favourite toys, while you will

While a bed does not serve the same purposes as a crate, it does provide the young puppy with a place to sleep. Place the dog's bed in a quiet corner of your family room.

enjoy the fact that they distract him from your expensive shoes and leather sofa. Puppies love to chew; in fact, chewing is a physical need for pups as they are teething, and everything looks appetising! The full range of your possessions—from old tea towel to Oriental carpet—are fair game in the eyes of a teething pup. Puppies are not all that discerning when it comes to finding something to literally 'sink their teeth into'—everything tastes great!

Only the safest, most durable toys should be offered to your puppy. Breeders advise owners to resist stuffed toys, because they can become de-stuffed in no time. The overly excited pup may ingest the stuffing, which is neither digestible nor nutritious.

Similarly, squeaky toys are quite popular, but must be avoided for the Lowchen. Perhaps a squeaky toy can be used as an aid in training, but not for free play. If a pup 'disembowels' one of these, the small plastic squeaker inside can be dangerous if swallowed. Monitor the condition of all your pup's toys carefully and get rid of any that

Even very young Lowchen puppies require something soft upon which to chew so they can assist their teeth in properly developing.

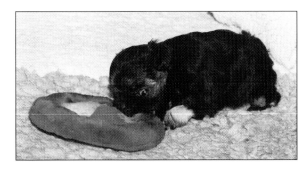

TOYS, TOYS, TOYS!

With a big variety of dog toys available, and so many that look like they would be a lot of fun for a dog, be careful in your selection. It is amazing what a set of puppy teeth can do to an innocent-looking toy, so, obviously, safety is a major consideration. Be sure to choose the most durable products that you can find. Hard nylon bones and toys are a safe bet, and many of them are offered in different scents and flavours that will be sure to capture your dog's attention. It is always fun to play a game of catch with your dog, and there are balls and flying discs that are specially made to withstand dog teeth.

have been chewed to the point of becoming potentially dangerous.

Be careful of natural bones, which have a tendency to splinter into sharp, dangerous pieces. Also be careful of rawhide, which can turn into pieces that are easy to swallow and become a mushy mess on your carpet.

LEAD

A nylon lead is probably the best option as it is the most resistant to puppy teeth should your pup take a liking to chewing on his lead. Of course, this is a habit that should be nipped in the bud, but if your pup likes to chew on his lead he has a very slim chance of being able to chew through the strong nylon. Nylon leads are also lightweight, which is good for a young Lowchen who is just getting used to the idea of walking on a lead. For everyday walking and safety purposes, the nylon lead is a good choice. As your pup grows up and gets used to walking on the lead, you may want to purchase a flexible lead. These leads allow you to extend the length to give the dog a broader area to explore or to shorten the length to keep the dog near you.

COLLAR

Your pup should get used to wearing a collar all the time since you will want to attach his ID tags to it. You have to attach the lead

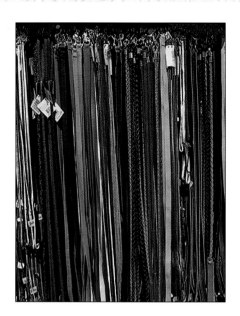

MENTAL AND DENTAL

Toys not only help your puppy get the physical and mental stimulation he needs but also provide a great way to keep his teeth clean. Hard rubber or nylon toys, especially those constructed with grooves, are designed to scrape away plaque, preventing bad breath and gum infection.

Your local pet shop will have a large variety of leads from which you may select one which best suits your needs.

PLAY'S THE THING

Teaching the puppy to play with his toys in running and fetching games is an ideal way to help the puppy develop muscle, learn motor skills and bond with you, his owner and master.

He also needs to learn how to inhibit his bite reflex and never to use his teeth on people, forbidden objects and other animals in play. Whenever you play with your puppy, you make the rules. This becomes an important message to your puppy in teaching him that you are the pack leader and control everything he does in life. Once your dog accepts you as his leader, your relationship with him will be cemented for life.

to something! A lightweight nylon collar is a good choice; make sure that it fits snugly enough so that the pup cannot wriggle out of it, but is loose enough so that it will not be uncomfortably tight around the pup's neck. You should be able to fit a finger between the pup and the collar. It may take some time for your pup to get used to wearing the collar, but soon he will not even notice that it is there.

CHOOSE AN APPROPRIATE COLLAR

The BUCKLE COLLAR is the standard collar used for everyday purpose. Be sure that you adjust the buckle on growing puppies. Check it every day. It can become too tight overnight! These collars can be made of leather or nylon. Attach your dog's identification tags to this collar.

The CHOKE COLLAR is the usual collar recommended for training, though not recommended for Toy and coated breeds. It is constructed of highly polished steel so that it slides easily through the stainless steel loop. The idea is that the dog controls the pressure around its neck and he will stop pulling if the collar becomes uncomfortable. Never leave a choke collar on your dog when not training.

The HALTER is for a trained dog that has to be restrained to prevent running away, chasing a cat and the like. Considered the most humane of all collars, it is frequently used on smaller dogs for which collars are not comfortable.

FOOD AND WATER BOWLS

Your pup will need two bowls, one for food and one for water. You may want two sets of bowls, one for inside and one for outside, depending on where the dog will be fed and where he will be spending time. Stainless steel or sturdy plastic bowls are popular choices. Plastic bowls are more chewable. Dogs tend not to chew on the steel variety, which can be sterilised. It is important to buy sturdy bowls since anything is in danger of being chewed by puppy teeth and you do not want your dog to be constantly chewing apart his bowl (for his safety and for your purse!).

CLEANING SUPPLIES

Until a pup is housetrained you will be doing a lot of cleaning. Accidents will occur, which is acceptable in the beginning because the puppy does not know any better. All you can do is be prepared to clean up any 'accidents.' Old rags, towels, newspapers and a safe disinfectant are good to have on hand.

BEYOND THE BASICS

The items previously discussed are the bare necessities. You will find out what else you need as you go along—grooming supplies, flea/tick protection, baby gates to partition a room, etc. These things will vary depending on your situation but it is important that

Bowls suitable for your Lowchen should be sturdily constructed and not too large.

PHOTO COURTESY OF MIKKI PET PRODUCTS.

Professional devices make the chore of cleaning up after your dog more manageable.

you have everything you need to feed and make your Lowchen comfortable in his first few days at home.

PUPPY-PROOFING YOUR HOME

Aside from making sure that your Lowchen will be comfortable in your home, you also have to make sure that your home is safe for your Lowchen. This means taking precautions that your pup will not get into anything he should not get into and that there is nothing within his reach that may harm him should he sniff it, chew it, inspect it, etc. This probably seems obvious since, while you

are primarily concerned with your pup's safety, at the same time you do not want your belongings to be ruined. Breakables should be placed out of reach if your dog is to have full run of the house. If he is to be limited to certain places within the house, keep any potentially dangerous items in the 'off-limits' areas. An electrical cord can pose a danger should the puppy decide to taste it—and who is going to convince a pup that it would not make a great chew toy? Cords should be fastened tightly against the wall. If your dog is going to spend time in a crate, make sure that there is nothing near his crate that he can reach if he sticks his curious little nose or paws through the openings. Just as you would with a child, keep all household cleaners and chemicals where the pup cannot reach them.

It is also important to make sure that the outside of your home

TOXIC PLANTS
Many plants can be toxic to dogs. If you see your dog carrying a piece of vegetation in his mouth, approach him in a quiet, disinterested manner, avoid eye contact, pet him and gradually remove the plant from his mouth. Alternatively, offer him a treat and maybe he'll drop the plant on his own accord. Be sure no toxic plants are growing in your own garden.

is safe. Of course your puppy should never be unsupervised, but a pup let loose in the garden will want to run and explore, and he should be granted that freedom. Do not let a fence give you a false sense of security; you would be surprised how crafty (and persistent) a dog can be in working out how to dig under and squeeze his way through small holes, or to jump or climb over a fence. The remedy is to make the fence well embedded into the ground and high enough so that it really is impossible for your dog to get over it. Be sure to repair or secure any gaps in the fence. Check the fence periodically to ensure that it is in good shape and make repairs as needed; a very determined pup may return to the same spot to 'work on it' until he is able to get through.

FIRST TRIP TO THE VET
You have selected your puppy, and your home and family are ready. Now all you have to do is

NATURAL TOXINS
Examine your grass and garden landscaping before bringing your puppy home. Many varieties of plants have leaves, stems or flowers that are toxic if ingested, and you can depend on a curious puppy to investigate them. Ask your vet for information on poisonous plants or research them at your library.

PUPPY-PROOFING
Thoroughly puppy-proof your house before bringing your puppy home. Never use roach or rodent poisons in any area accessible to the puppy. Avoid the use of toilet cleaners. Most dogs are born with 'toilet sonar' and will take a drink if the lid is left open. Also keep the rubbish secured and out of reach.

collect your Lowchen from the breeder and the fun begins, right? Well…not so fast. Something else you need to prepare is your pup's first trip to the veterinary surgeon. Perhaps the breeder can recommend someone in the area that specialises in Toy dogs, or maybe you know some other Lowchen owners who can suggest a good vet. Either way, you should have an appointment arranged for your pup before you pick him up.

The pup's first visit will consist of an overall examination to make sure that the pup does not have any problems that are not apparent to the owner. The veterinary surgeon will also set up a schedule for the pup's vaccinations; the breeder will inform you of which ones the pup has already received and the vet can continue from there.

INTRODUCTION TO THE FAMILY

Everyone in the house will be excited about the puppy coming home and will want to pet him

Do not overwhelm your Lowchen puppy the first day in its new home. Let the pup acclimate itself before meeting everyone in the neighbourhood!

and play with him, but it is best to make the introduction low-key so as not to overwhelm the puppy. He is apprehensive already. It is the first time he has been separated from his mother and the breeder, and the ride to your home is likely to be the first time he has been in a car. The last thing you want to do is smother him, as this will only frighten

HOW VACCINES WORK

If you've just bought a puppy, you surely know the importance of having your pup vaccinated, but do you understand how vaccines work? Vaccines contain the same bacteria or viruses that cause the disease you want to prevent, but they have been chemically modified so that they don't cause any harm. Instead, the vaccine causes your dog to produce antibodies that fight the harmful bacteria. Thus, if your pup is exposed to the disease in the future, the antibodies will destroy the viruses or bacteria.

him further. This is not to say that human contact is not extremely necessary at this stage, because this is the time when a connection between the pup and his human family is formed. Gentle petting and soothing words should help console him, as well as just putting him down and letting him explore on his

CHEMICAL TOXINS

Scour your garage for potential puppy dangers. Remove weed killers, pesticides and antifreeze materials. Antifreeze is highly toxic and even a few drops can kill an adult dog. The sweet taste attracts the animal, who will quickly consume it from the floor or curbside.

HOME WITH THE MANGE

Many young dogs suffer from demodectic mange, sometimes called red mange. While all breeds of dogs have suffered from demodectic mange, short-coated breeds are at a greater risk. The mange manifests itself as localised infections on the face, muzzle, neck and limbs. The symptoms include hair loss and red, scaly skin. Vets routinely treat demodectic mange so that secondary infections are avoided. Many breeders remove known carriers from their programmes.

own (under your watchful eye, of course).

The pup may approach the family members or may busy himself with exploring for a while. Gradually, each person should spend some time with the pup, one at a time, crouching down to get as close to the pup's level as possible and letting him sniff their hands and petting him gently. He definitely needs human attention and he needs to be touched—this is how to form an immediate bond. Just remember that the pup is experiencing a lot of things for the first time, at the same time. There are new people, new noises, new smells and new things to investigate: so be gentle, be affectionate and be as comforting as you can be.

PUP'S FIRST NIGHT HOME

You have travelled home with your new charge safely in his crate. He's been to the vet for a thorough check-up; he's been weighed, his papers examined; perhaps he's even been vaccinated and wormed as well. He's met the family, licked the whole family, including the excited children and the less-than-happy cat. He's explored his area, his new bed, the garden and anywhere else he's been permitted. He's eaten his first meal at home and relieved himself in the proper place. He's heard lots of new sounds, smelled new friends and seen more of the outside world than ever before.

That was just the first day! He's worn out and is ready for bed…or so you think!

It's puppy's first night and you are ready to say 'Good night'—

FEEDING TIP

You will probably start feeding your pup the same food that he has been getting from the breeder; the breeder should give you a few days' supply to start you off. Although you should not give your pup too many treats, you will want to have puppy treats on hand for coaxing, training, rewards, etc. Be careful, though, as a small pup's calorie requirements are relatively low and a few treats can add up to almost a full day's worth of calories without the required nutrition.

keep in mind that this is puppy's first night ever to be sleeping alone. His dam and littermates are no longer at paw's length and he's a bit scared, cold and lonely. Be reassuring to your new family member. This is not the time to spoil him and give in to his inevitable whining.

Puppies whine. They whine to let others know where they are and hopefully to get company out of it. Place your pup in his new bed or crate in his room and close the door. Mercifully, he may fall asleep without a peep. When the inevitable occurs, ignore the whining: he is fine. Be strong and keep his interest in mind. Do not allow yourself to feel guilty and visit the pup. He will fall asleep eventually.

Many breeders recommend placing a piece of bedding from his former home in his new bed so that he recognises the scent of his littermates. Others still advise placing a hot water bottle in his

bed for warmth. This latter may be a good idea provided the pup doesn't attempt to suckle—he'll get good and wet and may not fall asleep so fast.

Puppy's first night can be somewhat stressful for the pup and his new family. Remember that you are setting the tone of nighttime at your house. Unless you want to play with your pup every evening at 10 p.m., midnight and 2 a.m., don't initiate the habit. Your family will thank you, and so will your pup!

PREVENTING PUPPY PROBLEMS

SOCIALISATION

Now that you have done all of the preparatory work and have helped your pup get accustomed to his

Every dog must be socialised so they can properly interface with other dogs and people other than their masters and mistresses. This Lowchen is being greeted by a playful Griffon ready for a friendly game.

new home and family, it is about time for you to have some fun! Socialising your Lowchen pup gives you the opportunity to show off your new friend, and your pup gets to reap the benefits of being an adorable furry creature that people will want to pet and, in general, think is absolutely precious!

Besides getting to know his new family, your puppy should be exposed to other people, animals and situations, but of course he must not come into close contact with dogs you don't know well until his course of injections is fully complete. This will help him become well adjusted as he grows up and less prone to being timid or fearful of the new things he will encounter. Your pup's sociali-sation began with the breeder but now it is your responsibility to continue it. The socialisation he receives up until the age of 12 weeks is the most critical, as this is the time when he forms his impressions of the outside world. Be especially careful during the eight-to-ten-week period, also known as the fear period. The interaction he receives during this time should be gentle and reassuring. Lack of socialisation can manifest itself in fear and aggression as the dog grows up. He needs lots of human contact, affection, handling and exposure to other animals.

Once your pup has received his necessary vaccinations, feel free to take him out and about (on his lead, of course). Walk him around the neighbourhood, take him on your daily errands, let people pet him, let him meet other dogs and pets, etc. Puppies do not have to try to make friends; there will be no shortage of people who will want to introduce themselves. Just make sure that you carefully supervise each meeting. If the neighbourhood children want to say hello, for example, that is great— children and pups most often make great companions. Sometimes an excited child can unintentionally handle a pup too

Your Lowchen pup will enjoy spending time with his new owner and will soon develop a close bond to the members of his family.

MANNERS MATTER

During the socialisation process, a puppy should meet people, experience different environments and definitely be exposed to other canines. Through playing and interacting with other dogs, your puppy will learn lessons, ranging from controlling the pressure of his jaws by biting his littermates to the inner-workings of the canine pack that he will apply to his human relationships for the rest of his life. That is why removing a puppy from its litter too early (before eight weeks) can be detrimental to the pup's development.

roughly, or an overzealous pup can playfully nip a little too hard. You want to make socialisation experiences positive ones. What a pup learns during this very formative stage will affect his attitude toward future encounters. You want your dog to be comfortable around everyone. A pup that has a bad experience with a child may grow up to be a dog that is shy around or aggressive toward children.

CONSISTENCY IN TRAINING
Dogs, being pack animals, naturally need a leader, or else they try to establish dominance in their packs. When you

welcome a dog into your family, the choice of who becomes the leader and who becomes the 'pack' is entirely up to you! Your pup's intuitive quest for dominance, coupled with the fact that it is nearly impossible to look at an adorable Lowchen pup with his 'puppy-dog' eyes and not cave in, give the pup almost an unfair advantage in getting the upper hand! A pup will definitely test the waters to see what he can and cannot do. Do not give in to those pleading eyes—stand your ground when it comes to disciplining the pup and make sure that all family members do the same. It will only confuse the pup when Mother tells him to get off the sofa when he is used to sitting up there with Father to watch the nightly news. Avoid discrepancies by having all members of the

A FORTNIGHT'S GRACE
It will take at least two weeks for your puppy to become accustomed to his new surroundings. Give him lots of love, attention, handling, frequent opportunities to relieve himself, a diet he likes to eat and a place he can call his own.

SOCIALISATION
Thorough socialisation includes not only meeting new people but also being introduced to new experiences such as riding in the car, having his coat brushed, hearing the television, walking in a crowd—the list is endless. The more your pup experiences, and the more positive the experiences are, the less of a shock and the less frightening it will be for your pup to encounter new things.

household decide on the rules before the pup even comes home…and be consistent in enforcing them! Early training shapes the dog's personality, so you cannot be unclear in what you expect.

COMMON PUPPY PROBLEMS
The best way to prevent puppy problems is to be proactive in stopping an undesirable behaviour as soon as it starts. The old saying 'You can't teach an old dog new tricks' does not necessarily hold true, but it is

PROPER SOCIALISATION

The socialisation period for puppies is from age 8 to 16 weeks. This is the time when puppies need to leave their birth family and take up residence with their new owners, where they will meet many new people, other pets, etc. Failure to be adequately socialised can cause the dog to grow up fearing others and being shy and unfriendly due to a lack of self-confidence.

true that it is much easier to discourage bad behaviour in a young developing pup than to wait until the pup's bad behaviour becomes the adult dog's bad habit. There are some problems that are especially prevalent in puppies as they develop.

NIPPING

As puppies start to teethe, they feel the need to sink their teeth into anything available...unfortunately that includes your fingers, arms, hair and toes. You may find this behaviour cute for the first five seconds...until you feel just how sharp those puppy teeth are. This is something you want to discourage immediately and consistently with a firm 'No!' (or whatever number of firm 'No's' it

THE RIDE HOME

Taking your dog from the breeder to your home in a car can be a very uncomfortable experience for both of you. The puppy will have been taken from his warm, friendly, safe environment and brought into a strange new environment. An environment that moves! Be prepared for loose bowels, urination, crying, whining and even fear biting. With proper love and encouragement when you arrive home, the stress of the trip should quickly disappear.

takes for him to understand that you mean business). Then replace your finger with an appropriate chew toy. While this behaviour is merely annoying when the dog is young, it can become harmful as your Lowchen's adult teeth grow in and his jaws develop, and he continues to think it is okay to gnaw on human appendages. Your Lowchen does not mean any harm with a friendly nip, but he also does not know his own strength.

CRYING/WHINING

Your pup will often cry, whine, whimper, howl or make some type of commotion when he is left alone. This is basically his way of calling out for attention to make sure that you know he is there and that you have not forgotten about him. He feels

PUPPY PROBLEMS

The majority of problems that are commonly seen in young pups will disappear as your dog gets older. However, how you deal with problems when he is young will determine how he reacts to discipline as an adult dog. It is important to establish who is boss (hopefully it will be you!) right away when you are first bonding with your dog. This bond will set the tone for the rest of your life together.

CHEWING TIPS

Chewing goes hand in hand with nipping in the sense that a teething puppy is always looking for a way to soothe his aching gums. In this case, instead of chewing on you, he may have taken a liking to your favourite shoe or something else which he should not be chewing. Again, realise that this is a normal canine behaviour that does not need to be discouraged, only redirected. Your pup just needs to be taught what is acceptable to chew on and what is off limits. Consistently tell him 'NO' when you catch him chewing on something forbidden and give him a chew toy. Conversely, praise him when you catch him chewing on something appropriate. In this way you are discouraging the inappropriate behaviour and reinforcing the desired behaviour. The puppy chewing should stop after his adult teeth have come in, but an adult dog continues to chew for various reasons—perhaps because he is bored, perhaps to relieve tension or perhaps he just likes to chew. That is why it is important to redirect his chewing when he is still young.

Lowchens depend on their owners for interaction and affection. While some Lowchens are independent free-thinkers, most Lowchens prefer to be close to their people.

TRAINING TIP
Training your dog takes much patience and can be frustrating at times, but you should see results from your efforts. If you have a dog that seems untrainable, take him to a trainer or behaviourist. The dog may have a personality problem that requires the help of a professional, or perhaps you need help in learning how to train your dog.

crate with cosy bedding and a toy comes in handy. You want to know that he is safe when you are not there to supervise, and you know that he will be safe in his crate rather than roaming freely about the house. In order for the pup to stay in his crate without making a fuss, he needs to be comfortable in his crate. On that note, it is extremely important that the crate is never used as a form of punishment, or the pup will have a negative association with the crate.

Accustom the pup to the crate in short, gradually increasing time intervals in which you put him in the crate, maybe with a treat, and stay in the room with him. If he cries or makes a fuss, do not go to him, but stay in his sight. Gradually he will realise that staying in his crate is all right without your help, and it will not be so traumatic for him when you are not around. You may want to leave the radio on softly when you leave the house; the sound of human voices may be comforting to him.

insecure when he is left alone, when you are out of the house and he is in his crate or when you are in another part of the house and he cannot see you. The noise he is making is an expression of the anxiety he feels at being alone, so he needs to be taught that being alone is okay. You are not actually training the dog to stop making noise, you are training him to feel comfortable when he is alone and thus removing the need for him to make the noise. This is where the

NO CHOCOLATE!
Use treats to bribe your dog into a desired behaviour. Try small pieces of hard cheese or freeze-dried liver. Never offer chocolate as it has toxic qualities for dogs.

FEEDING TIP
You must store your dried dog food carefully. Open packages of dog food quickly lose their vitamin value, usually within 90 days of being opened. Mould spores and vermin could also contaminate the food.

DIETARY AND FEEDING CONSIDERATIONS

Today the choices of food for your Lowchen are many and varied. There are simply dozens of brands of food in all sorts of flavours and textures, ranging from puppy diets to those for seniors. There are even hypoallergenic and low-calorie diets available. Because your Lowchen's food has a bearing on coat, health and temperament, it is essential that the most suitable diet is selected for a Lowchen of his age. It is fair to say, however, that even experienced owners can be perplexed by the enormous range of foods available. Only understanding what is best for your dog will help you reach a valued decision.

Dog foods are produced in three basic types: dried, semi-moist and tinned. Dried foods are useful for the cost-conscious, for overall they tend to be less expensive than semi-moist or tinned. They also contain the least fat and the most preservatives. In general, tinned foods are made up of 60–70 percent water, while semi-moist ones often contain so much sugar that they are perhaps the least preferred by owners, even though their dogs seem to like them.

When selecting your dog's diet, three stages of development must be considered: the puppy stage, adult stage and the senior or veteran stage.

PUPPY STAGE

Puppies instinctively want to suck milk from their mother's teats and a normal puppy will exhibit this behaviour from just a few moments following birth. If puppies do not attempt to suckle within the first half-hour or so, they should be encouraged to do so by placing them on the nipples, having selected ones with plenty of milk. This early milk supply is important in providing colostrum to protect the puppies during the first eight to ten weeks of their lives. Although a mother's milk is much better than any milk formula, despite there being some excellent ones available, if the puppies do not feed, the breeder will have to feed them himself. For those with less experience, advice from a veterinary surgeon is important so that breeders feed not only the right quantity of milk but that of correct quality, fed at suitably frequent intervals, usually every two hours during the first few days of life.

Puppies should be allowed to nurse from their mothers for about

FOOD PREFERENCE
Selecting the best dried dog food is difficult. There is no majority consensus among veterinary scientists as to the value of nutrient analyses (protein, fat, fibre, moisture, ash, cholesterol, minerals, etc.). All agree that feeding trials are what matter, but you also have to consider the individual dog. Its weight, age, activity and what pleases its taste all must be considered. It is probably best to take the advice of your veterinary surgeon. Every dog's dietary requirements vary, even during the lifetime of a particular dog.

If your dog is fed a good dried food, it does not require supplements of meat or vegetables. Dogs do appreciate a little variety in their diets so you may choose to stay with the same brand, but vary the flavour. Alternatively, you may wish to add a little flavoured stock to give a difference to the taste.

the first six weeks, although from the third or fourth week the breeder should begin to introduce small portions of suitable solid food. Most breeders like to introduce alternate milk and meat meals initially, building up to weaning time.

By the time the puppies are seven or a maximum of eight

Puppies are weaned to solid food by the eighth week. Discuss what food brands the breeder uses for the puppies and resume with these same brands when you take your Lowchen home.

THE CANINE GOURMET

Your dog does not prefer a fresh bone. Indeed, he wants it properly aged and, if given such a treat indoors, he is more likely to try to bury it in the carpet than he is to settle in for a good chew! If you have a garden, give him such delicacies outside and guide him to a place suitable for his 'bone yard.' He will carefully place the treasure in its earthy vault and seemingly forget about it. Trust me, his seeming distaste or lack of thanks for your thoughtfulness is not that at all. He will return in a few days to inspect it, perhaps to re-bury the thing, and when it is just right, he will relish it as much as you do that cooked-to-perfection steak. If he is in a concrete or bricked kennel run, he will be especially frustrated at the hopelessness of the situation. He will vacillate between ignoring it completely, giving it a few licks to speed the curing process with saliva, and trying to hide it behind the water bowl! When the bone has aged a bit, he will set to work on it.

weeks old, they should be fully weaned and fed solely on a proprietary puppy food. Selection of the most suitable, good-quality diet at this time is essential, for a puppy's fastest growth rate is during the first year of life. Veterinary surgeons are usually able to offer advice in this regard. The frequency of meals will be reduced over time, and change of diet should be followed according to the manufacturer's instructions and the vet's advice.

Puppy and junior diets should be well balanced for the needs of your dog, so that except in certain circumstances additional vitamins, minerals and proteins will not be required.

ADULT DIETS

A dog is considered an adult when it has stopped growing, so in general the diet of a Lowchen can be changed to an adult one at about eight to ten months of age, sometimes sooner depending on one's selection of diet. There are many specially prepared diets available, and it is important that you select the food best suited to your dog's needs. Lowchens are active dogs, and are therefore likely to require a higher protein content in their diets than those leading a more sedate life. If your Lowchen has been spayed or neutered, has been seriously ill or is elderly, you should take your vet's advice as to the best diet to feed.

TEST FOR PROPER DIET

A good test for proper diet is the colour, odour and firmness of your dog's stool. A healthy dog usually produces three semi-hard stools per day. The stools should have no unpleasant odour. They should be the same colour from excretion to excretion.

SENIOR DIETS

As dogs get older, their metabolism changes. The older dog usually exercises less, moves more slowly and sleeps more. This change in lifestyle and physiological performance requires a change in diet. Since these changes take place slowly, they might not be recognisable. What is easily recognisable is weight gain. By continuing to feed your dog an adult-maintenance diet when it is slowing down metabolically, your dog will gain weight. Obesity in an older dog compounds the health problems that already accompany old age.

As your dog gets older, few of his organs function up to par. The kidneys slow down and the intestines become less efficient. These age-related factors are best handled with a change in diet and a change in feeding schedule to give smaller portions that are more easily digested.

There is no single best diet for every older dog. While many dogs do well on light or senior diets, other dogs do better on puppy diets or other special premium diets such as lamb and rice. Be sensitive to your senior Lowchen's diet and this will help control other problems that may arise with your old friend.

WATER

Just as your dog needs proper nutrition from his food, water is

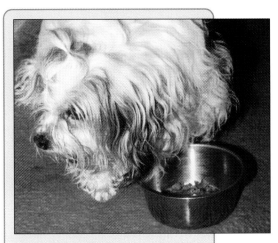

GRAIN-BASED DIETS

Some less expensive dog foods are based on grains and other plant proteins. While these products may appear to be attractively priced, many breeders prefer a diet based on animal proteins and believe that they are more conducive to your dog's health. Many grain-based diets rely on soy protein that may cause flatulence (passing gas).

There are many cases, however, when your dog might require a special diet. These special requirements should only be recommended by your veterinary surgeon.

an essential 'nutrient' as well. Water keeps the dog's body properly hydrated and promotes normal function of the body's systems. During toilet training it is necessary to keep an eye on how much water your Lowchen is drinking, but once he is reliably trained he should have access to

DRINK, DRANK, DRUNK—
MAKE IT A DOUBLE

In both humans and dogs, as well as most living organisms, water forms the major part of nearly every body tissue. Naturally, we take water for granted, but without it, life as we know it would cease.

For dogs, water is needed to keep their bodies functioning biochemically. Additionally, water is needed to replace the water lost while panting. Unlike humans who are able to sweat to dissipate heat, dogs must pant to cool down, thereby losing the vital water from their bodies needed to regulate their body temperatures. Humans lose electrolyte-containing products and other body-fluid components through sweating; dogs do not lose anything except water.

Water is essential always, but especially so when the weather is hot or humid or when your dog is exercising or working vigorously.

clean fresh water at all times, especially if you feed dried food. Make certain that the dog's water bowl is clean, and change the water often.

EXERCISE

All dogs require exercise and the lively and energetic Lowchen is certainly no exception. A sedentary lifestyle is as harmful to a dog as it is to a person. The Lowchen, an active Toy breed, needs to be walked regularly and enjoys supervised free play in the garden. Bear in mind that an overweight dog should never be suddenly over-exercised; instead he should be encouraged to increase exercise slowly.

It is important to realise that not only is exercise essential to keep the dog's body fit, it is essential to his mental well-being. A bored dog will find something to do, which often manifests itself in some type of destructive behaviour. In this sense, exercise is essential for the owner's mental well-being as well!

GROOMING

Firstly it is important to realise that although the Lowchen's coat may look like that of a lion, it does not grow that way naturally—it has to be cared for. Some parts of the coat are trimmed, with other parts left to grow naturally with no trimming whatsoever.

WHAT ARE YOU FEEDING YOUR DOG?

Read the label on your dog food. Many dog foods only advise what 50–55% of the contents are, leaving the other 45% in doubt.

Calcium 1.3%

Fatty Acids 1.6%

Crude Fibre 4.6%

Moisture 11%

Crude Fat 14%

Crude Protein 22%

45.5% ? ? ?

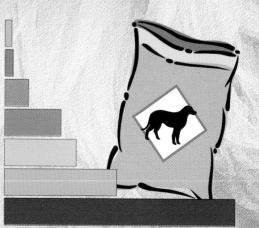

FEEDING TIPS

Dog food must be at room temperature, neither too hot nor too cold. Fresh water, changed daily and served in a clean bowl, is mandatory, especially when feeding dried food.

Never feed your dog from the table while you are eating. Never feed your dog leftovers from your own meal. They usually contain too much fat and too much seasoning.

Dogs must chew their food. Hard pellets are excellent; soups and slurries are to be avoided.

Don't add left-overs or any extras to normal dog food. The normal food is usually balanced and adding something extra destroys the balance.

Except for age-related changes, dogs do not require dietary variations. They can be fed the same diet, day after day, without their becoming ill.

Your Lowchen will need to be groomed regularly, so it is essential that short grooming sessions be introduced from a very early age. From the very beginning a few minutes each day should be set aside, the duration building up slowly as the puppy matures and the coat grows in length. Most Lowchen owners begin to trim their puppies' coats into lion trims from around four or five weeks of age, using either portable clippers or standard pet clippers. The clippers will make a noise, so it is a good idea for your youngster to be allowed to hear the sound of clippers a few times before his first experience with

'DOES THIS COLLAR MAKE ME LOOK FAT?'

While humans may obsess about how they look and how trim their bodies are, many people believe that extra weight on their dogs is a good thing. The truth is, pets should not be over- or under-weight, as both can lead to or signal sickness. In order to tell how fit your pet is, run your hands over his ribs. Are his ribs buried under a layer of fat or are they sticking out considerably? If your pet is within his normal weight range, you should be able to feel the ribs easily. If you stand above him, the outline of his body should resemble an hourglass. Some breeds do tend to be leaner while some are a bit stockier, but making sure your dog is the right weight for his breed will certainly contribute to his good health.

GROOMING EQUIPMENT

Narrow-toothed metal comb
Wide-toothed metal comb
Pin brush
Clippers with #30 and #15 blades
Bristle brush
Pet clippers (if required)
Hair-dryer
Dog shampoo
Dog conditioner
Rubber mat
Towels
Nail clippers
Shower or shower attachment
Liquid ear cleaner
Tissues/cotton wool
Tooth cleaning aid

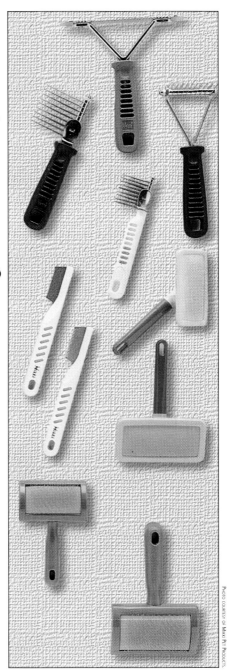

Your local pet shop will have the necessary grooming tools with which you can keep your Lowchen looking like a tidy little lion dog.

PHOTO COURTESY OF MIKKI PET PRODUCTS.

them. At first a puppy will wonder why it feels somewhat 'unclothed' around its back end, but soon it will grow used to this feeling and will not even bat an eyelid.

Your puppy should be taught to stand on a solid surface for grooming, a suitable table on which he will not slip. Under no circumstances should you leave your Lowchen alone on a table, for he may all too easily jump off, which would be dangerous. When the puppy is used to standing on the table, you will probably find it useful to teach him to be rolled over onto his side. Do this by grasping his front and back legs on the opposite side of your own body, then gently placing him down by leaning over him for reassurance. To begin with, just stroke his tummy so that he looks upon this new routine as something highly pleasurable. Then, when you know he is comfortable, introduce a few soft brush strokes. Be sure not to hurt him at all at this stage, for this would cause him to associate the grooming routine with pain. This may take a little getting used to both for you and your puppy, but if your Lowchen learns to lie down on his side you will more easily be able to groom in all the awkward places. You will both be glad you had a little patience to learn this trick from the very start!

Owners who keep their Lowchens as pets rather than for show will still need to pay attention to the coat on a daily basis, but some owners also like to take their dogs to a professional

Coat conditioners come in spray bottles and are most helpful when grooming the Lowchen. It is much easier to groom the hair when it is moist.

> **EXERCISE ALERT!**
> You should be careful where you exercise your dog. Many countryside areas have been sprayed with chemicals that are highly toxic to both dogs and humans. Never allow your dog to eat grass or drink from puddles on either public or private grounds, as the run-off water may contain chemicals from sprays and herbicides.

groomer every few weeks.

All owners will have favourite ways of grooming their dogs, and hopefully other owners with whom you come into contact will freely pass on some of their tips.

TRIMMING

Trimming is done when the coat is dry and, generally, about every two weeks. However, in the height of the show season trimming is usually done more regularly. To get the very best effect, most exhibitors like to trim their Lowchens a couple of days before a show.

To trim a Lowchen, your set of clippers will need to be fitted with a #30 blade for the body and front legs. Many breeders prefer to use a #15 blade or a portable pet trimmer for the feet. Feet are trimmed up to where the dewclaws would be, with the feet left looking small and round, as is required in the breed standard. Most owners like also to trim between the pads for, apart from the aspect of neatness, long hair can all too easily build up between the pads and cause painful knots beneath the feet. This, therefore, is not an area that should ever be neglected.

To leave 'bracelets' of coat on all four legs, trimming on the front legs starts again from above the area where the dewclaws would have been. The front legs should then be trimmed up to the elbow. On the hind legs, trimming is done from the hocks right up the hindquarters to the point at which the last rib can be felt. The lower half of the tail is trimmed also, leaving a plume of hair at the end.

PRESENTING THE LONG COAT

The Lowchen's long areas of coat are brushed out to give them an appearance of fullness, although one should always keep in mind that this is a single-coated breed. The coat should therefore never look so dense as on one of the Tibetan breeds, for example, where a double coat is needed as insulation against the cold. The body coat often parts naturally so that it falls evenly on either side of the body; it should never be parted artificially.

Keep in mind that to prevent coat breakage, a fine water or

A Lowchen trio on a grooming table, illustrating how confident dogs feel on a non-slip surface.

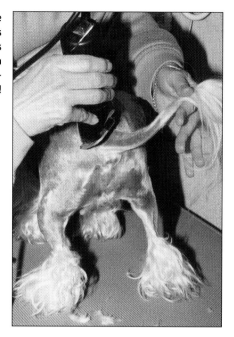

Clipping the Lowchen's hindquarters to give him that distinctive lion rear!

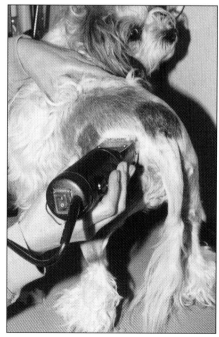

Skill in using an electric dog clipper requires experience and patience. It is best to have an experienced groomer show you the proper way to hold and angle the clipper before attempting to clip your Lowchen.

conditioning spray should always be used when grooming the coat through; the coat should never be combed or brushed when completely dry. Many owners like to use a pure bristle brush for the finishing touches.

Long ear fringes are highly prized, so care should be taken especially on these. They should absolutely not be trimmed into shape...that would be sacrilege! Hair on the head should always be kept clean; most people like to use a fine-toothed comb around the eye areas so that there is no build-up from the small amount of discharge that can come from the eyes. Eyes should always be kept clean, and although in some countries owners trim around their Lowchens' eyes, this is not done in Britain. After all, there should be no real need for trimming around the eyes.

The Lowchen should have large, round, intelligent eyes. Before going into the show ring the hair is combed backward over the skull so that, although it falls naturally, the eyes can be fully seen. The fine-toothed comb is also useful for keeping the beard clean, and this area can be wiped down with a dampened cloth after each meal to prevent soilage.

BATHING AND DRYING

How frequently you decide to bath your Lowchen will depend very much on whether yours is a show dog or a pet. Show dogs are usually bathed before every show, which may be as frequent as once a week. Pet dogs are usually bathed less frequently.

As with grooming, every owner has his or her own preference as to how best to bath, but ideally the coat should have been groomed through before bathing. I like to stand my own dogs on a non-slip mat in the bath, then wet the coat thoroughly using a shower. It is imperative that the water temperature is tested on your own hand before wetting the dog's coat.

Use a good quality shampoo designed especially for dogs. Always stroke the shampoo into the coat rather than rub, so as not to create knots. When the shampoo has been thoroughly rinsed out, apply a canine conditioner in the same manner and then rinse again until the water runs clear. Many people like to use a baby shampoo on the head to avoid irritation to the eyes, and some like to plug the ears with cotton wool to avoid water getting inside them. Personally, I use neither of these; I have just taken special care in those areas and have never encountered problems.

Finally, lift your Lowchen carefully out of the bath, wrapped in a clean towel. Undoubtedly your dog will want to shake—so be prepared! Drying can be done

The way a Lowchen is clipped greatly affects the way it is perceived in the show ring. Be certain to have a correct picture of the Lowchen in mind before turning on the clippers.

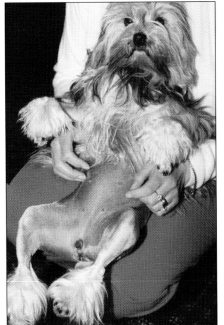

Grooming comes naturally to the Lowchen. This little chap proudly displays his smooth belly.

Wet the coat thoroughly before applying the shampoo. Be careful not to get water in the Lowchen's delicate eyes or ears.

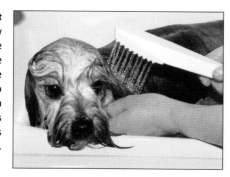

Apply the shampoo and massage it thoroughly into the dog's coat.

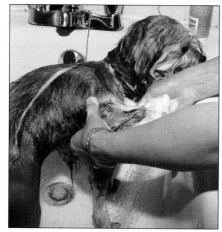

After rinsing out the shampoo, use a heavy towel to absorb the excess water from the dog's coat. Be prepared for the dog to shake when you remove the towel.

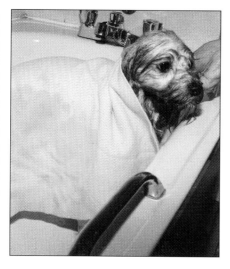

SOAP IT UP
The use of human soap products like shampoo, bubble bath and hand soap can be damaging to a dog's coat and skin. Human products are too strong and remove the protective oils coating the dog's hair and skin (that make him water-resistant). Use only shampoo made especially for dogs and you may like to use a medicated shampoo, which will always help to keep external parasites at bay.

on the same table that you use for the grooming process. Work systematically, applying warm air from the hair-dryer, using your comb or pin brush to help separate the hair as it dries. Brush the coat forward from the last rib, making sure that the coat nearest the skin is dry before moving on to the next section.

EAR CLEANING
Hair will grow inside the Lowchen's ears. This should be carefully plucked out from an early age, either using your fingers or blunt-ended tweezers. There is now available a powder to help make hair removal easier; this is usually available from larger or high-quality pet outlets. Remove only a few hairs at a time and the process should be entirely painless.

Ears must always be kept clean. This can be done using a special liquid cleaner with cotton wool. Many people use cotton wool buds, but their use is discouraged as it is easy to delve into the ears and cause injury.

Be on the lookout for any signs of infection or ear mite infestation. If your Lowchen has been shaking his head or scratching at his ears frequently, this usually indicates a problem. If his ears have an unusual odour, this is a sure sign of mite infestation or infection, and a signal to have his ears checked by the veterinary surgeon.

Nail Clipping

Your Lowchen should be accustomed to having his nails

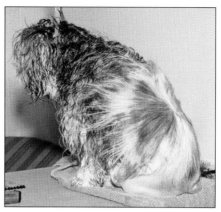

A hair dryer or blaster should be used to assist in the drying of the coat. Be careful not to burn the dog's skin—keep the blaster a foot or more from the dog's coat.

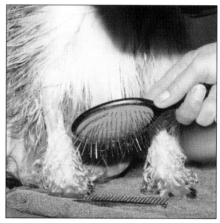

A pin brush and comb should be used as the hot air is drying the coat.

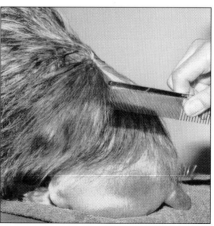

BATHING BEAUTY

Once you are sure that the dog is thoroughly rinsed, squeeze the excess water out of the coat with your hand and dry him with a heavy towel. You should finish the drying process with a hair-dryer. In cold weather, never allow your dog outside with a wet coat.

There are 'dry bath' products on the market, which are sprays and powders intended for spot cleaning, that can be used between regular baths, if necessary. They are not substitutes for regular baths, but they are easy to use for touch-ups as they do not require rinsing.

Do not leave the Lowchen on the grooming table unattended.

Pluck the long hairs protruding from the dog's ears.

Be very careful when combing around the Lowchen's eyes.

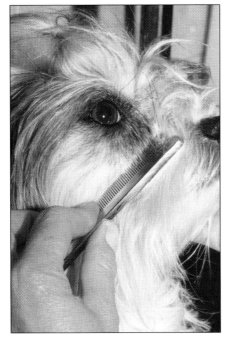

trimmed at an early age, since it will be part of your maintenance routine throughout his life. Long nails are uncomfortable for any dog and can scratch someone unintentionally. Also, a long nail has a better chance of ripping and bleeding, or causing the feet to spread. A good rule of thumb is that if you can hear your dog's nails clicking on the floor when he walks, his nails are too long.

Before you start cutting, make sure you can identify the

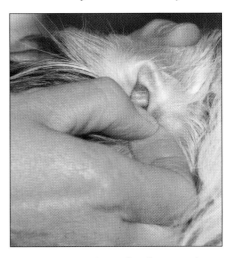

'quick' in each nail. The quick is a blood vessel that runs through the centre of each nail and grows rather close to the end. It will bleed if accidentally cut, which will be quite painful for the dog as it contains nerve endings. Keep some type of clotting agent on hand, such as a styptic pencil or styptic powder (the type used for shaving). This will stop the bleeding quickly when applied to the end of the cut nail. Do not panic if you cut the quick, just stop the bleeding and talk soothingly to your dog. Once he has calmed down, move on to the next nail. It is better to clip a little at a time, particularly with black-nailed dogs.

Hold your pup steady as you begin trimming his nails; you do not want him to make any sudden movements or run away. Talk to him soothingly and stroke him as you clip. Holding his foot in your hand, simply take off the end of each nail in one quick clip. You can purchase nail clippers that are specially made for dogs; you can probably find them wherever you buy pet or grooming supplies.

TRAVELLING WITH YOUR DOG

CAR TRAVEL

You should accustom your Lowchen to riding in a car at an early age. You may or may not take him in the car often, but at the very least he will need to go to the vet and you do not want these trips to be traumatic for the dog or troublesome for you. The safest way for a dog to ride in the car is in his crate. If he uses a crate in the house, you can use the same crate for travel.

Put the pup in the crate and see how he reacts. If he seems uneasy, you can have a passenger hold him on his lap while you

The hair around the feet must be closely trimmed to give the Lowchen a tidy appearance.

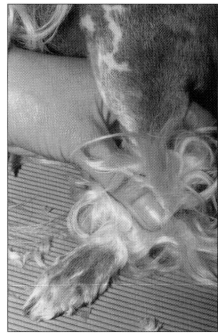

Begin clipping your puppy's nails at an early age. Soon he will accept nail clipping as a regular part of the grooming session.

Nail Maintenance

Nail Casing

Quick

Cut Line

Dark-Coloured Nails

With black or dark nails, where the quick is not easy to see, it's best to clip only the tip of the nail or to use a file.

Light-Coloured Nails

In light-coloured nails, clipping is much simpler because you can see the vein (or quick) that grows inside the casing.

drive. Another option is a specially made safety harness for dogs, which straps the dog in much like a seat belt. Do not let the dog roam loose in the vehicle—this is very dangerous! If you should stop short, your dog can be thrown and injured. If the dog starts climbing on you and pestering you while you are

PEDICURE TIP

A dog that spends a lot of time outside on a hard surface, such as cement or pavement, will have his nails naturally worn down and may not need to have them trimmed as often, except maybe in the colder months when he is not outside as much. Regardless, it is best to get your dog accustomed to this procedure at an early age so that he is used to it. Some dogs are especially sensitive about having their feet touched, but if a dog has experienced it since he was young, he should not be bothered by it.

TRAVEL TIP
Never leave your dog alone in the car. In hot weather your dog can die from the high temperature inside a closed vehicle; even a car parked in the shade can heat up very quickly. Leaving the window open is dangerous as well since the dog can hurt himself trying to get out.

driving, you will not be able to concentrate on the road. It is an unsafe situation for everyone—human and canine.

For long trips, be prepared to stop to let the dog relieve himself. Take with you whatever you need to clean up after him, including some paper kitchen towels and perhaps some old towelling for use should he have an accident in the car or suffer from travel sickness.

AIR TRAVEL

While it is possible to take a dog on a flight within Britain, this is fairly unusual and advance permission is always required. The dog will be required to travel in a fibreglass crate and you should always check in advance with the airline regarding specific requirements. To help the dog be at ease, put one of his favourite toys in the crate with him. Do not feed the dog for at least six hours before the trip to minimise his need to relieve himself. However,

certain regulations specify that water must always be made available to the dog in the crate.

Make sure your dog is properly identified and that your contact information appears on his ID tags and on his crate. Animals travel in a different area

The safest way to transport your Lowchen in the car is by using his crate. The same crate you use indoors can be used for travelling.

ON THE ROAD
If you are going on a long motor trip with your dog, be sure the hotels are dog friendly. Many hotels do not accept dogs. Also take along some ice that can be thawed and offered to your dog if he becomes overheated. Most dogs like to lick ice.

> **VACCINATIONS**
> For international travel you will have to make arrangements well in advance (perhaps months), as countries' regulations pertaining to bringing in animals differ. There may be special health certificates and/or vaccinations that your dog will need before taking the trip; sometimes this has to be done within a certain time frame. In rabies-free countries, you will need to bring proof of the dog's rabies vaccination and there may be a quarantine period upon arrival.

of the plane than human passengers so every rule must be strictly followed so as to prevent the risk of getting separated from your dog.

BOARDING
So you want to take a family holiday—and you want to include all members of the family. You would probably make arrangements for accommodation ahead of time anyway, but this is especially important when travelling with a dog. You do not want to make an overnight stop at the only place around for miles and find out that they do not allow dogs. Also, you do not want to reserve a place for your family without confirming that you are travelling with a dog because if it is against their policy you may not have a place to stay.

Alternatively, if you are travelling and choose not to bring your Lowchen, you will have to make arrangements for him while you are away. Some options are to take him to a neighbour's house to stay while you are gone, to have a trusted neighbour pop in often or stay at your house or to bring your dog to a reputable boarding kennel. If you choose to board him at a kennel, you should visit in advance to see the facilities provided, how clean they are and where the dogs are kept. Talk to some of the employees and see how they treat the dogs—have they experience in grooming small, long-coated dogs, do they spend time with the dogs, play with them, exercise them, etc.? Also find out the kennel's policy on vaccinations and what they require. This is for all of the dogs'

> **TRAVEL TIP**
> The most extensive travel you do with your dog may be limited to trips to the veterinary surgeon's office—or you may decide to bring him along for long distances when the family goes on holiday. Whichever the case, it is important to consider your dog's safety while travelling.

safety, since when dogs are kept together, there is a greater risk of diseases being passed from dog to dog.

IDENTIFICATION
Your Lowchen is your valued companion and friend. That is why you always keep a close eye on him and you have made sure that he cannot escape from the garden or wriggle out of his collar and run away from you. However, accidents can happen and there may come a time when your dog unexpectedly gets separated from you. If this unfortunate event should occur, the first thing on your mind will be finding him. Proper identification, including an

ID tag, a tattoo, and possibly a microchip, will increase the chances of his being returned to you safely and quickly.

Exercise pens (or ex-pens) are handy for travelling to dog shows, as they give the dog an opportunity to stretch his legs within the safe confines of the pen.

Living with an untrained dog is a lot like owning a piano that you do not know how to play—it is a nice object to look at but it does not do much more than that to bring you pleasure. Now try taking piano lessons and suddenly the piano comes alive and brings forth magical sounds and rhythms that set your heart singing and your body swaying.

The same is true with your Lowchen. Any dog is a big responsibility and if not trained sensibly may develop unaccept-able behaviour that annoys you or could even cause family friction.

To train your Lowchen, you may like to enrol in an obedience class. Teach him good manners as you learn how and why he behaves the way he does. Find out how to communicate with your dog and how to recognise and understand his communications with you. Suddenly the dog takes on a new role in your life—he is clever, interesting, well-behaved and fun to be with. He demonstrates his bond of devotion to you daily. In other words, your Lowchen does wonders for your ego because he constantly reminds you that you are not only his leader, you are his hero!

Those involved with teaching dog obedience and counselling owners about their dogs' behaviour have discovered some interesting facts about dog ownership. For example, training dogs when they are puppies results in the highest rate of success in developing well-mannered and well-adjusted adult dogs. Training an older dog, from six months to six years of age, can produce almost equal results providing that the owner accepts the dog's slower rate of learning capability and is willing to work patiently to help the dog succeed at developing to his fullest potential. Unfortunately, many owners of untrained adult dogs lack the patience factor, so they

THE HAND THAT FEEDS
To a dog's way of thinking, your hands are like his mouth in terms of a defence mechanism. If you squeeze him too tightly, he might just bite you because that would be his normal response. This is not aggressive biting and, although all biting should be discouraged, you need the discipline in learning how to handle your dog.

PARENTAL GUIDANCE
Training a dog is a life experience. Many parents admit that much of what they know about raising children they learned from caring for their dogs. Dogs respond to love, fairness and guidance, just as children do. Become a good dog owner and you may become an even better parent.

do not persist until their dogs are successful at learning particular behaviours.

Training a puppy aged 10 to 16 weeks (20 weeks at the most) is like working with a dry sponge in a pool of water. The pup soaks up whatever you show him and constantly looks for more things to do and learn. At this early age, his body is not yet producing hormones, and therein lies the reason for such a high rate of success. Without hormones, he is focused on his owners and not particularly interested in investigating other places, dogs, people, etc. You are his leader: his provider of food, water, shelter and security. He latches onto you and wants to stay close. He will usually follow you from room to room, will not let you out of his sight when you are outdoors with him and will respond in like manner to the people and animals you encounter. If you greet a friend warmly, he will be happy

to greet the person as well. If, however, you are hesitant, even anxious, about the approach of a stranger, he will respond accordingly.

Once the puppy begins to produce hormones, his natural curiosity emerges and he begins to investigate the world around him. It is at this time when you may notice that the untrained dog begins to wander away from you

REAP THE REWARDS
If you start with a normal, healthy dog and give him time, patience and some carefully executed lessons, you will reap the rewards of that training for the life of the dog. And what a life it will be! The two of you will find immeasurable pleasure in the companionship you have built together with love, respect and understanding.

and even ignore your commands to stay close. When this behaviour becomes a problem, the owner has two choices: get rid of the dog or train him. It is strongly urged that you choose the latter option.

There are usually classes within a reasonable distance from the owner's home, but you can also do a lot to train your dog yourself. Sometimes there are classes available but the tuition is too costly. Whatever the circumstances, the solution to the problem of lack of lesson availability lies within the pages of this book.

This chapter is devoted to helping you train your Lowchen at home. If the recommended procedures are followed faithfully, you may expect positive results that will prove rewarding both to you and your dog.

Whether your new charge is a puppy or a mature adult, the methods of teaching and the

THINK BEFORE YOU BARK
Dogs are sensitive to their master's moods and emotions. Use your voice wisely when communicating with your dog. Never raise your voice at your dog unless you are angry and trying to correct him. 'Barking' at your dog can become as meaningless as 'dogspeak' is to you. Think before you bark!

techniques we use in training basic behaviours are the same. After all, no dog, whether puppy or adult, likes harsh or inhumane methods. All creatures, however, respond favourably to gentle motivational methods and sincere praise and encouragement. Now let us get started.

TOILET TRAINING

You can train a puppy to relieve itself wherever you choose, but this must be somewhere suitable. You should bear in mind from the outset that when your puppy is old enough to go out in public places, any canine deposits must be removed at once. You will always have to carry with you a small plastic bag or 'poop-scoop.'

Outdoor training includes such surfaces as grass, soil and cement. Indoor training usually means training your dog to newspaper.

When deciding on the surface

MEALTIME
Mealtime should be a peaceful time for your puppy. Do not put his food and water bowls in a high-traffic area in the house. For example, give him his own little corner of the kitchen where he can eat undisturbed and where he will not be underfoot. Do not allow small children or other family members to disturb the pup when he is eating.

TRAINING TIP

Dogs will do anything for your attention. If you reward the dog when he is calm and resting, you will develop a well-mannered dog. If, on the other hand, you greet your dog excitedly and encourage him to wrestle with you, the dog will greet you the same way and you will have a hyperactive dog on your hands.

and location that you will want your Lowchen to use, be sure it is going to be permanent. Training your dog to grass and then changing your mind two months later is extremely difficult for both dog and owner.

Next, choose the command you will use each and every time you want your puppy to void. 'Hurry up' and 'Toilet' are examples of commands commonly used by dog owners.

Get in the habit of giving the puppy your chosen relief command before you take him out. That way, when he becomes an adult, you will be able to determine if he wants to go out when you ask him. A confirmation will be signs of interest, wagging his tail, watching you intently, going to the door, etc.

PUPPY'S NEEDS

Puppy needs to relieve himself after play periods, after each meal, after he has been sleeping and at any time he indicates that he is looking for a place to urinate or defecate.

HONOUR AND OBEY

Dogs are the most honourable animals in existence. They consider another species (humans) as their own. They interface with you. You are their leader. Puppies perceive children to be on their level; their actions around small children are different from their behaviour around their adult masters.

If you have any ambitions of eventually showing your Lowchen, it must be trained at an early age to pose properly for a judge's evaluation.

The urinary and intestinal tract muscles of very young puppies are not fully developed. Therefore, like human babies, puppies need to relieve themselves frequently.

Take your puppy out often—every hour for an eight-week-old, for example, and always immediately after sleeping and eating.

TAKE THE LEAD

Do not carry your dog to his toilet area. Lead him there on a leash or, better yet, encourage him to follow you to the spot. If you start carrying him to his spot, you might end up doing this routine forever and your dog will have the satisfaction of having trained YOU.

THE GOLDEN RULE

The golden rule of dog training is simple. For each 'question' (command), there is only one correct answer (reaction). One command = one reaction. Keep practising the command until the dog reacts correctly without hesitating. Be repetitive but not monotonous. Dogs get bored just as people do!

The older the puppy, the less often he will need to relieve himself. Finally, as a mature healthy adult, he will require only three to five relief trips per day.

HOUSING

Since the types of housing and control you provide for your

puppy have a direct relationship on the success of housetraining, we consider the various aspects of both before we begin training.

Taking a new puppy home and turning him loose in your house can be compared to turning a child loose in a sports arena and telling the child that the place is all his! The sheer enormity of the place would be too much for him to handle.

Instead, offer the puppy clearly defined areas where he can play, sleep, eat and live. A room of the house where the family gathers is the most obvious choice. Puppies are social animals and need to feel a part of the pack right from the start. Hearing your voice, watching you while you are doing things and smelling you nearby are all positive reinforcers that he is now a member of your pack. Usually a family room, the kitchen or a nearby adjoining breakfast area is ideal for providing safety and security for both puppy and owner.

COMMAND STANCE
Stand up straight and authoritatively when giving your dog commands. Do not issue commands when lying on the floor or lying on your back on the sofa. If you are on your hands and knees when you give a command, your dog will think you are positioning yourself to play.

PRACTICE MAKES PERFECT!
• Have training lessons with your dog every day in several short segments—three to five times a day for a few minutes at a time is ideal.
• Do not have long practice sessions. The dog will become easily bored.
• Never practise when you are tired, ill, worried or in an otherwise negative mood. This will transmit to the dog and may have an adverse effect on its performance.

Think fun, short and above all POSITIVE! End each session on a high note, rather than a failed exercise, and make sure to give a lot of praise. Enjoy the training and help your dog enjoy it, too.

Within that room there should be a smaller area that the puppy can call his own. An alcove, a wire or fibreglass dog crate or a fenced (not boarded!) corner from which he can view the activities of his new family will be fine. The size of the area or crate is the key factor here. The area must be large enough for the puppy to lie down and stretch out as well as stand up without rubbing his head on the top, yet small enough so that he cannot relieve himself at one end and sleep at the other without coming into contact with his droppings until fully trained to relieve himself outside.

Dogs are, by nature, clean animals and will not remain close

to their relief areas unless forced to do so. In those cases, they then become dirty dogs and usually remain that way for life.

The designated area should contain clean bedding and a toy. Water must always be available, in a non-spill container.

CONTROL

By control, we mean helping the puppy to create a lifestyle pattern that will be compatible to that of his human pack (YOU!). Just as we guide little children to learn our way of life, we must show the puppy when it is time to play, eat, sleep, exercise and even entertain himself.

Your puppy should always sleep in his crate. He should also learn that, during times of household confusion and excessive human activity such as at breakfast when family members are preparing for the day, he can play by himself in relative safety and comfort in his designated area. Each time you leave the puppy alone, he should understand exactly where he is to stay. Puppies are chewers. They cannot tell the difference between lamp cords, television wires, shoes, table legs, etc. Chewing into a television wire, for example, can be fatal to the puppy while a shorted wire can start a fire in the house.

If the puppy chews the arm of the chair when he is alone, you will probably discipline him angrily when you get home. Thus, he makes the association that your coming home means he is going to be punished. (He will not remember chewing the chair and is incapable of making the association of the discipline with his naughty deed.)

Other times of excitement, such as family parties, etc., can be fun for the puppy providing he can view the activities from the security of his designated area. He is not underfoot and he is not being fed all sorts of titbits that will probably cause him stomach distress, yet he still feels a part of the fun.

CANINE DEVELOPMENT SCHEDULE

It is important to understand how and at what age a puppy develops into adulthood. If you are a puppy owner, consult the following Canine Development Schedule to determine the stage of development your puppy is currently experiencing. This knowledge will help you as you work with the puppy in the weeks and months ahead.

Period	Age	Characteristics
FIRST TO THIRD	BIRTH TO SEVEN WEEKS	Puppy needs food, sleep and warmth, and responds to simple and gentle touching. Needs mother for security and disciplining. Needs littermates for learning and interacting with other dogs. Pup learns to function within a pack and learns pack order of dominance. Begin socialising with adults and children for short periods. Begins to become aware of its environment.
FOURTH	EIGHT TO TWELVE WEEKS	Brain is fully developed. Needs socialising with outside world. Remove from mother and littermates. Needs to change from canine pack to human pack. Human dominance necessary. Fear period occurs between 8 and 12 weeks. Avoid fright and pain.
FIFTH	THIRTEEN TO SIXTEEN WEEKS	Training and formal obedience should begin. Less association with other dogs, more with people, places, situations. Period will pass easily if you remember this is pup's change-to-adolescence time. Be firm and fair. Flight instinct prominent. Permissiveness and over-disciplining can do permanent damage. Praise for good behaviour.
JUVENILE	FOUR TO EIGHT MONTHS	Another fear period about 7 to 8 months of age. It passes quickly, but be cautious of fright and pain. Sexual maturity reached. Dominant traits established. Dog should understand sit, down, come and stay by now.

NOTE: THESE ARE APPROXIMATE TIME FRAMES. ALLOW FOR INDIVIDUAL DIFFERENCES IN PUPPIES.

SCHEDULE

A puppy should be taken to his relief area each time he is released from his designated area, after meals, after a play session and when he first awakens in the morning (at age eight weeks, this can mean 5 a.m.!). The puppy will indicate that he's ready 'to go' by circling or sniffing busily—do not misinterpret these signs. For a puppy less than ten weeks of age, a routine of taking him out every hour is

THE SUCCESS METHOD

Success that comes by luck is usually short lived. Success that comes by well-thought-out proven methods is often more easily achieved and permanent. This is the Success Method. It is designed to give you, the puppy owner, a simple yet proven way to help your puppy develop clean living habits and a feeling of security in his new environment.

THE SUCCESS METHOD

1 Tell the puppy 'Crate time!' and place him in the crate with a small treat (a piece of cheese or half of a biscuit). Let him stay in the crate for five minutes while you are in the same room. Then release him and praise lavishly. Never release him when he is fussing. Wait until he is quiet before you let him out.

2 Repeat Step 1 several times a day.

3 The next day, place the puppy in the crate as before. Let him stay there for ten minutes. Do this several times.

4 Continue building time in five-minute increments until the puppy

stays in his crate for 30 minutes with you in the room. Always take him to his relief area after prolonged periods in his crate.

5 Now go back to Step 1 and let the puppy stay in his crate for five minutes, this time while you are out of the room.

6 Once again, build crate time in five-minute increments with you out of the room. When the puppy will stay willingly in his crate (he may even fall asleep!) for 30 minutes with you out of the room, he will be ready to stay in it for several hours at a time.

6 Steps to Successful Crate Training

necessary. As the puppy grows, he will be able to wait for longer periods of time.

Keep trips to his relief area short. Stay no more than five or six minutes and then return to the house. If he goes during that time, praise him lavishly and take him indoors immediately. If he does not, but he has an accident when you go back indoors, pick him up immediately, say 'No! No!' and return to his relief area. Wait a few minutes, then return to the house again. Never hit a puppy or rub his face in urine or excrement when he has had an accident!

Once indoors, put the puppy in his crate until you have had time to clean up his accident. Then release him to the family area and watch him more closely than before. Chances are, his

HOW MANY TIMES A DAY?

AGE	RELIEF TRIPS
To 14 weeks	10
14–22 weeks	8
22–32 weeks	6
Adulthood	4
(dog stops growing)	

These are estimates, of course, but they are a guide to the MINIMUM opportunities a dog should have each day to relieve itself.

THE CLEAN LIFE

By providing sleeping and resting quarters that fit the dog, and offering frequent opportunities to relieve himself outside his quarters, the puppy quickly learns that the outdoors (or the newspaper if you are training him to paper) is the place to go when he needs to urinate or defecate. It also reinforces his innate desire to keep his sleeping quarters clean. This, in turn, helps develop the muscle control that will eventually produce a dog with clean living habits.

accident was a result of your not picking up his signal or waiting too long before offering him the opportunity to relieve himself. Never hold a grudge against the puppy for accidents.

Let the puppy learn that going outdoors means it is time to relieve himself, not play. Once trained, he will be able to play indoors and out and still differentiate between the times for play versus the times for relief.

Help him develop regular hours for naps, being alone, playing by himself and just resting, all in his crate. Encourage him to entertain himself while you are busy with your activities. Let him learn that having you near is comforting, but it is not your main purpose in life to provide him with undivided attention.

Each time you put a puppy in his own area, use the same command, whatever suits best. Soon he will run to his crate or special area when he hears you say those words.

Crate training provides safety for you, the puppy and the home. It also provides the puppy with a feeling of security, and that helps the puppy achieve self-confidence and clean habits.

Remember that one of the primary ingredients in housetraining your puppy is control. Regardless of your lifestyle, there will always be occasions when you will need to have a place where your dog can stay and be happy and safe. Crate training is the answer for now and in the future.

In conclusion, a few key elements are really all you need for a successful housetraining method—consistency, frequency, praise, control and supervision. By following these procedures with a normal, healthy puppy, you and the puppy will soon be past the stage of 'accidents' and ready to move on to a full and rewarding life together.

TRAINING RULES
If you want to be successful in training your dog, you have four rules to obey yourself:
1. Develop an understanding of how a dog thinks.
2. Do not blame the dog for lack of communication.
3. Define your dog's personality and act accordingly.
4. Have patience and be consistent.

ROLES OF DISCIPLINE, REWARD AND PUNISHMENT
Discipline, training one to act in accordance with rules, brings order to life. It is as simple as that. Without discipline, particularly in a group society, chaos reigns supreme and the group will eventually perish. Humans and canines are social animals and need some form of discipline in order to function effectively. They must procure food, protect their home base and their young and reproduce to keep the species going.

If there were no discipline in the lives of social animals, they would eventually die from starvation and/or predation by other stronger animals.

In the case of domestic canines, dogs need discipline in their lives in order to understand how their pack (you and other family members) functions and how they must act in order to survive.

A large humane society in a highly populated area recently surveyed dog owners regarding their satisfaction with their relationships with their dogs. People who had trained their dogs were 75% more satisfied with their pets than those who had never trained their dogs.

Dr Edward Thorndike, a psychologist, established *Thorndike's Theory of Learning*, which states that a behaviour that results in a pleasant event tends to be repeated. A behaviour that results in an unpleasant event tends not to be repeated. It is this theory on which training methods are based today. For example, if you manipulate a dog to perform a

PAPER CAPER
Never line your pup's sleeping area with newspaper. Puppy litters are usually raised on newspaper and, once in your home, the puppy will immediately associate newspaper with voiding. Never put newspaper on any floor while housetraining, as this will only confuse the puppy. If you are paper-training him, use paper in his designated relief area ONLY. Finally, restrict water intake after evening meals. Offer a few licks at a time—never let a young puppy gulp water after meals.

HOUSETRAINING TIP
Most of all, be consistent. Always take your dog to the same location, always use the same command, and always have him on lead when he is in his relief area, unless a fenced-in garden is available.

By following the Success Method, your puppy will be completely housetrained by the time his muscle and brain development reach maturity. Keep in mind that small breeds usually mature faster than large breeds, but all puppies should be trained by six months of age.

Always clean up after your Lowchen, whether you're in a public place or in your own garden.

specific behaviour and reward him for doing it, he is likely to do it again because he enjoyed the end result.

Occasionally, punishment, a penalty inflicted for an offence, is necessary. The best type of punishment often comes from an outside source. For example, a

child is told not to touch the stove because he may get burned. He disobeys and touches the stove. In doing so, he receives a burn. From that time on, he respects the heat of the stove and avoids contact with it. Therefore, a behaviour that results in an unpleasant event tends not to be repeated.

A good example of a dog learning the hard way is the dog who chases the house cat. He is told many times to leave the cat alone, yet he persists in teasing the cat. Then, one day he begins chasing the cat but the cat turns and swipes a claw across the dog's face, leaving him with a painful gash on his nose. The final result is that the dog stops chasing the cat.

TRAINING EQUIPMENT

COLLAR AND LEAD
For a Lowchen the collar and lead that you use for training must be one with which you are easily able to work, not too heavy for the dog and perfectly safe.

TREATS

Have a bag of treats on hand. Something nutritious and easy to swallow works best. Use a soft treat, a chunk of cheese or a piece of cooked chicken rather than a dry biscuit. By the time the dog has finished chewing a dry treat, he will forget why he is being rewarded in the first place! Using food rewards will not teach a dog to beg at the table—the only way to teach a dog to beg at the table is to give him food from the table. In training, rewarding the dog with a food treat will help him associate praise and the treats with learning new behaviours that obviously please his owner.

TRAINING BEGINS: ASK THE DOG A QUESTION

In order to teach your dog anything, you must first get his attention. After all, he cannot learn anything if he is looking away from you with his mind on something else.

To get his attention, ask him, 'School?' and immediately walk over to him and give him a treat as you tell him 'Good dog.' Wait a minute or two and repeat the routine, this time with a treat in your hand as you approach within a foot of the dog. Do not go directly to him, but stop about a foot short of him and hold out the treat as you ask, 'School?' He will see you approaching with a treat in your hand and most likely

begin walking toward you. As you meet, give him the treat and praise again.

The third time, ask the question, have a treat in your hand and walk only a short distance toward the dog so that he must walk almost all the way to

SAFETY FIRST

While it may seem that the most important things to your dog are eating, sleeping and chewing the upholstery on your furniture, his first concern is actually safety. The domesticated dogs we keep as companions have the same pack instinct as their ancestors who ran free thousands of years ago. Because of this pack instinct, your dog wants to know that he and his pack are not in danger of being harmed, and that his pack has a strong, capable leader. You must establish yourself as the leader early on in your relationship. That way your dog will trust that you will take care of him and the pack, and he will accept your commands without question.

to a series of sounds for him, and those sounds become the signal to go to you and pay attention; if he does, he will get to interact with you plus receive treats and praise.

THE BASIC COMMANDS

TEACHING SIT

Now that you have the dog's attention, attach his lead and hold it in your left hand and a food treat in your right. Place your food hand at the dog's nose and let him lick the treat but not take it from you. Say 'Sit' and slowly raise your food hand from in front of the dog's nose up over his head so that he is looking at the ceiling. As he bends his head upward, he will have to bend his knees to maintain his balance. As he bends his knees, he will assume a sit position. At that point, release the food treat and praise lavishly with comments such as 'Good dog! Good sit!,' etc. Remember to always praise enthusiastically, because dogs relish verbal praise from their owners and feel so proud of themselves whenever they accomplish a behaviour.

You will not use food forever in getting the dog to obey your commands. Food is only used to teach new behaviours, and once the dog knows what you want when you give a specific command, you will wean him off the food treats but still maintain the verbal praise. After all, you

OPEN MINDS
Dogs are as different from each other as people are. What works for one dog may not work for another. Have an open mind. If one method of training is unsuccessful, try another.

you. As he reaches you, give him the treat and praise again.

By this time, the dog will probably be getting the idea that if he pays attention to you, especially when you ask that question, it will pay off in treats and enjoyable activities for him. In other words, he learns that 'school' means doing great things with you that are fun and result in positive attention for him.

Remember that the dog does not understand your verbal language; he only recognises sounds. Your question translates will always have your voice with you, and there will be many times when you have no food rewards but expect the dog to obey.

Teaching Down

Teaching the down exercise is easy when you understand how the dog perceives the down position, and it is very difficult when you do not. Dogs perceive the down position as a submissive one, therefore teaching the down exercise using a forceful method can sometimes make the dog develop such a fear of the down that he either runs away when you say 'Down' or he attempts to snap at the person who tries to force him down.

Have the dog sit close alongside your left leg, facing in the same direction as you are. Hold the lead in your left hand and a food treat in your right. Now place your left hand lightly on the top of the dog's shoulders where they meet above the spinal cord. Do not push down on the dog's shoulders; simply rest your left hand there so you can guide the dog to lie down close to your left leg rather than to swing away from your side when he drops.

Now place the food hand at the dog's nose, say 'Down' very softly (almost a whisper), and slowly lower the food hand to the dog's front feet. When the food hand reaches the floor, begin moving it forward along the floor

FEAR AGGRESSION

Pups who are subjected to physical abuse during training commonly end up with behavioural problems as adults. One common result of abuse is fear aggression, in which a dog will lash out, bare his teeth, snarl and finally bite someone by whom he feels threatened. For example, your daughter may be playing with the dog one afternoon. As they play hide-and-seek, she backs the dog into a corner, and as she attempts to tease him playfully, he bites her hand. Examine the cause of this behaviour. Did your daughter ever hit the dog? Did someone who resembles your daughter hit or scream at the dog? Fortunately, fear aggression is relatively easy to correct. Have your daughter engage in only positive activities with the dog, such as feeding, petting and walking. She should not give any corrections or negative feedback. If the dog still growls or cowers away from her, allow someone else to accompany them. After approximately one week, the dog should feel that he can rely on her for many positive things, and he will also be prevented from reacting fearfully towards anyone who might resemble her.

DOUBLE JEOPARDY

A dog in jeopardy never lies down. He stays alert on his feet because instinct tells him that he may have to run away or fight for his survival. Therefore, if a dog feels threatened or anxious, he will not lie down. Consequently, it is important to have the dog calm and relaxed as he learns the down exercise.

in front of the dog. Keep talking softly to the dog, saying things like, 'Do you want this treat? You can do this, good dog.' Your reassuring tone of voice will help calm the dog as he tries to follow the food hand in order to get the treat.

When the dog's elbows touch the floor, release the food and praise softly. Try to get the dog to maintain that down position for several seconds before you let him sit up again. The goal here is to get the dog to settle down and not feel threatened in the down position.

Teaching Stay

It is easy to teach the dog to stay in either a sit or a down position. Again, we use food and praise during the teaching process as we help the dog to understand exactly what it is that we are expecting him to do.

To teach the sit/stay, start with the dog sitting on your left side as before and hold the lead in your left hand. Have a food treat in your right hand and place your food hand at the dog's nose. Say 'Stay' and step out on your right foot to stand directly in front of the dog, toe to toe, as he licks and nibbles the treat. Be sure to keep his head facing upward to maintain the sit position. Count to five and then swing around to stand next to the dog again with him on your left. As soon as you get back to the original position, release the food and praise lavishly.

To teach the down/stay, do the down as previously described. As soon as the dog lies down, say 'Stay' and step out on your right foot just as you did in the sit/stay. Count to five and then return to stand beside the dog with him on your left side. Release the treat and praise as always.

Within a week or ten days, you can begin to add a bit of distance between you and your

FAMILY TIES

If you have other pets in the home and/or interact often with the pets of friends and other family members, your pup will respond to those pets in much the same manner as you do. It is only when you show fear of or resentment toward another animal that he will act fearful or unfriendly.

OBEDIENCE SCHOOL
Taking your dog to an obedience school may be the best investment in time and money you can ever make. You will enjoy the benefits for the lifetime of your dog and you will have the opportunity to meet people with your similar expectations for companion dogs.

dog when you leave him. When you do, use your left hand open with the palm facing the dog as a stay signal, much the same as the hand signal a constable uses to stop traffic at an intersection. Hold the food treat in your right hand as before, but this time the food is not touching the dog's nose. He will watch the food hand and quickly learn that he is going to get that treat as soon as you return to his side.

When you can stand 1 metre away from your dog for 30 seconds, you can then begin building time and distance in both stays. Eventually, the dog can be expected to remain in the stay position for prolonged periods of time until you return to him or call him to you. Always praise lavishly when he stays.

Teaching Come

If you make teaching 'come' an exciting experience, you should never have a 'student' that does not love the game or that fails to come when called. The secret, it seems, is never to teach the word 'come.'

At times when an owner most wants his dog to come when called, the owner is likely to be upset or anxious and he allows these feelings to come through in the tone of his voice when he calls his dog. Hearing that desperation in his owner's voice, the dog fears the results of going to him and therefore either disobeys outright or runs in the opposite direction. The secret, therefore, is to teach the dog a game and, when you want him to come to you, simply play the game. It is practically a no-fail solution!

To begin, have several members of your family take a few food treats and each go into a

CONSISTENCY PAYS OFF
Dogs need consistency in their feeding schedule, exercise and toilet breaks and in the verbal commands you use. If you use 'Stay' on Monday and 'Stay here, please' on Tuesday, you will confuse your dog. Don't demand perfect behaviour during training classes and then let him have the run of the house the rest of the day. Above all, lavish praise on your pet consistently every time he does something right. The more he feels he is pleasing you, the more willing he will be to learn.

'WHERE ARE YOU?'

When calling the dog, do not say 'Come.' Say things like, 'Rover, where are you? See if you can find me! I have a biscuit for you!' Keep up a constant line of chatter with coaxing sounds and frequent questions such as, 'Where are you?' The dog will learn to follow the sound of your voice to locate you and receive his reward.

different room in the house. Take turns calling the dog, and each person should celebrate the dog's finding him with a treat and lots of happy praise. When a person calls the dog, he is actually inviting the dog to find him and get a treat as a reward for 'winning.'

A few turns of the 'Where are you?' game and the dog will understand that everyone is playing the game and that each person has a big celebration awaiting his success at locating them. Once he learns to love the game, simply calling out 'Where are you?' will bring him running from wherever he is when he hears that all-important question.

The come command is recognised as one of the most important things to teach a dog, but there are trainers who work with thousands of dogs and never teach the actual word 'Come.' Yet

these dogs will race to respond to a person who uses the dog's name followed by 'Where are you?' For example, a woman has a 12-year-old companion dog who went blind, but who never fails to locate her owner when asked, 'Where are you?'

Children, in particular, love to play this game with their dogs. Children can hide in smaller places like a shower or bath, behind a bed or under a table. The dog needs to work a little bit harder to find these hiding places, but when he does he loves to celebrate with a treat and a tussle with a favourite youngster.

TEACHING HEEL

Heeling means that the dog walks beside the owner without pulling. It takes time and patience on the owner's part to succeed at teaching the dog that he (the owner) will not proceed unless the dog is walking calmly beside him. Pulling out ahead on the

'COME' ... BACK

Never call your dog to come to you for a correction or scold him when he reaches you. That is the quickest way to turn a 'Come' command into 'Go away fast!' Dogs think only in the present tense, and your dog will connect the scolding with coming to you, not with the misbehaviour of a few moments earlier.

TRAINING TIP
If you are walking your dog and he suddenly stops and looks straight into your eyes, ignore him. Pull the leash and lead him into the direction you want to walk.

Show dogs are trained to heel at their owner's side. A show dog pulling at the lead would not show off his gait to his best advantage.

lead is definitely not acceptable.

Begin by holding the lead in your left hand as the dog sits beside your left leg. Move the loop end of the lead to your right hand but keep your left hand short on the lead so it keeps the dog in close next to you.

Say 'Heel' and step forward on your left foot. Keep the dog close to you and take three steps. Stop and have the dog sit next to you in what we now call the 'heel position.' Praise verbally, but do not touch the dog. Hesitate a moment and begin again with 'Heel,' taking three steps and stopping, at which point the dog is told to sit again.

Your goal here is to have the dog walk those three steps without pulling on the lead. Once he will walk calmly beside you for three steps without pulling, increase the number of steps you take to five. When he will walk politely beside you while you take five steps, you can increase the length of your walk to ten steps. Keep increasing the length of your stroll until the dog will walk quietly beside you without

pulling as long as you want him to heel. When you stop heeling, indicate to the dog that the exercise is over by verbally praising as you pet him and say 'OK, good dog.' The 'OK' is used as a release word meaning that the exercise is finished and the dog is free to relax.

If you are dealing with a dog who insists on pulling you around, simply 'put on your brakes' and stand your ground

HEELING WELL
Teach your dog to HEEL in an enclosed area. Once you think the dog will obey reliably and you want to attempt advanced obedience exercises such as off-lead heeling, test him in a fenced-in area so he cannot run away.

dog will begin to respond and within a few days he will be walking politely beside you without pulling on the lead. At first, the training sessions should be kept short and very positive; soon the dog will be able to walk nicely with you for increasingly longer distances. Remember also to give the dog free time and the opportunity to run and play when you have finished heel practice.

WEANING OFF FOOD IN TRAINING

Food is used in training new behaviours. Once the dog understands what behaviour goes with a specific command, it is time to start weaning him off the food treats. At first, give a treat after each exercise. Then, start to give a treat only after every other exercise. Mix up the times when you offer a food reward and the times when you only offer praise so that the dog will never know when he is going to receive both food and praise and when he is going to receive only praise. This is called a variable ratio reward system and it proves successful because there is always the chance that the owner will produce a treat, so the dog never stops trying for that reward. No matter what, ALWAYS give verbal praise.

OBEDIENCE CLASSES

It is a good idea to enrol in an obedience class if one is available

Treats are an effective way of getting a dog's attention, although they should only be used when teaching new commands. Practise without treats once the dog has learned the command.

until the dog realises that the two of you are not going anywhere until he is beside you and moving at your pace, not his. It may take some time just standing there to convince the dog that you are the leader and you will be the one to decide on the direction and speed of your travel.

Each time the dog looks up at you or slows down to give a slack lead between the two of you, quietly praise him and say, 'Good heel. Good dog.' Eventually, the in your area. If yours is a show dog, ringcraft classes would be more appropriate. Many areas have dog clubs that offer basic obedience training as well as preparatory classes for obedience competition. There are also local dog trainers who offer similar classes.

At dog shows, dogs can earn titles at various levels of competition. The beginning levels of competition include basic behaviours such as sit, down, heel, etc. The more advanced levels of competition include jumping, retrieving, scent discrimination and signal work. The advanced levels require a dog and owner to put a lot of time and effort into their training and the titles that can be earned at these levels of competition are very prestigious.

KEEP SMILING
Never train your dog, puppy or adult, when you are angry or in a sour mood. Dogs are very sensitive to human feelings, especially anger, and if your dog senses that you are angry or upset, he will connect your anger with his training and learn to resent or fear his training sessions.

OTHER ACTIVITIES FOR LIFE
Whether a dog is trained in the structured environment of a class or alone with his owner at home, there are many activities that can bring fun and rewards to both owner and dog once they have mastered basic control.

Teaching the dog to help out around the home, in the garden or on the farm provides great satisfaction to both dog and owner. In addition, the dog's help makes life a little easier for his owner and raises his stature as a valued companion to his family. It helps give the dog a purpose by occupying his mind and providing an outlet for his energy.

If you are interested in participating in organised competition with your Lowchen, there are activities other than obedience in which you and your dog can become involved. Agility is a popular sport where dogs run through an obstacle course that includes various jumps, tunnels and other exercises to test the dog's speed and coordination. Mini-agility has been devised by The Kennel Club for small breeds to participate. The events are essentially the same except all obstacles have been reduced in size. The owners run beside their dogs to give commands and to guide them through the course. Although competitive, the focus is on fun—it's fun to do, fun to watch and great exercise.

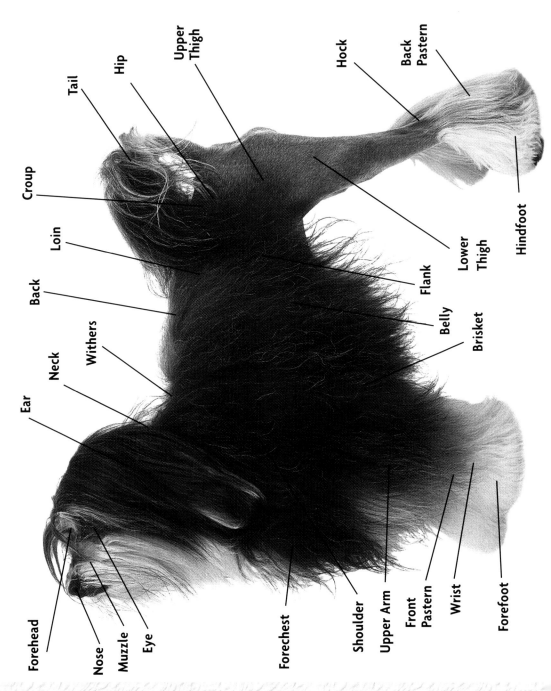

PHYSICAL STRUCTURE OF THE LOWCHEN

Health Care of Your

LOWCHEN

Dogs suffer from many from of the same physical illnesses as people. They might even share many of the same psychological problems. Since people usually know more about human diseases than canine maladies, many of the terms used in this chapter will be familiar but not necessarily those used by veterinary surgeons. We will use the term *x-ray*, instead of the more acceptable term *radiograph*. We will also use the familiar term *symptoms* even though dogs don't have symptoms, which are verbal descriptions of the patient's feelings; dogs have *clinical signs*. Since dogs can't speak, we have to look for clinical signs...but we still use the term *symptoms* in this book.

As a general rule, medicine is *practised*. That term is not arbitrary. Medicine is a constantly changing art as we learn more and more about genetics, electronic aids (like CAT scans) and daily laboratory advances. There are many dog maladies, like canine hip dysplasia, which are not universally treated in the same manner. Some veterinary surgeons opt for surgery more often than others do.

SELECTING A VETERINARY SURGEON
Your selection of a veterinary surgeon should not be based upon personality (as most are) but upon their convenience to your home. You want a vet who is close because you might have emergencies or need to make multiple visits for treatments. You want a vet who has services that you might require such as tattooing and grooming, as well as sophisticated pet supplies and a good reputation for ability and responsiveness. There is nothing more frustrating than having to wait a day or more to get a response from your veterinary surgeon.

All veterinary surgeons are licensed and their diplomas and/or certificates should be displayed in their waiting rooms. There are, however, many veterinary specialities that usually require further studies and internships. There are specialists in heart problems (veterinary cardiologists), skin problems (veterinary dermatologists), teeth and gum problems (veterinary dentists), eye problems (veterinary ophthalmologists) and x-rays (veterinary radiologists), as well as vets who have specialities in

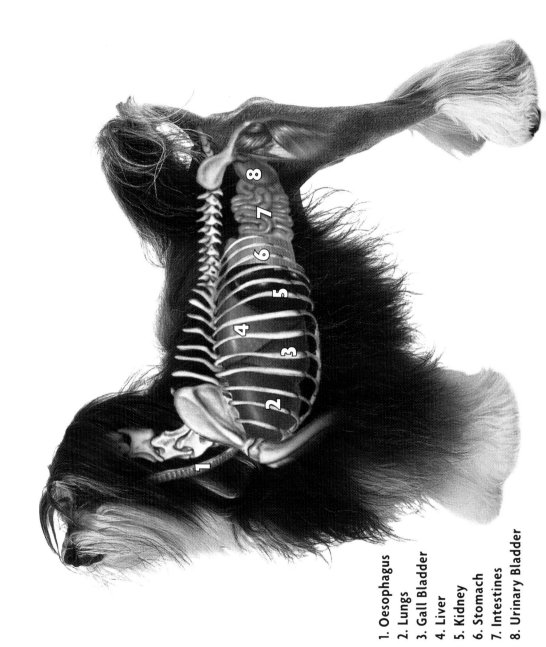

1. Oesophagus
2. Lungs
3. Gall Bladder
4. Liver
5. Kidney
6. Stomach
7. Intestines
8. Urinary Bladder

INTERNAL ORGANS OF THE LOWCHEN

bones, muscles or other organs. Most veterinary surgeons do routine surgery such as neutering, stitching up wounds and docking tails for those breeds in which such is required for show purposes. When the problem affecting your dog is serious, it is not unusual or impudent to get another medical opinion, although in Britain you are obliged to advise the vets concerned about this. You might also want to compare costs among several veterinary surgeons.

Breakdown of Veterinary Income by Category

2%	Dentistry
4%	Radiology
12%	Surgery
15%	Vaccinations
19%	Laboratory
23%	Examinations
25%	Medicines

DISEASE REFERENCE CHART

	What is it?	What causes it?	Symptoms
Leptospirosis	Severe disease that affects the internal organs; can be spread to people.	A bacterium, which is often carried by rodents, that enters through mucous membranes and spreads quickly throughout the body.	Range from fever, vomiting and loss of appetite in less severe cases to shock, irreversible kidney damage and possibly death in most severe cases.
Rabies	Potentially deadly virus that infects warm-blooded mammals. Not seen in United Kingdom.	Bite from a carrier of the virus, mainly wild animals.	1st stage: dog exhibits change in behaviour, fear. 2nd stage: dog's behaviour becomes more aggressive. 3rd stage: loss of coordination, trouble with bodily functions.
Parvovirus	Highly contagious virus, potentially deadly.	Ingestion of the virus, which is usually spread through the faeces of infected dogs.	Most common: severe diarrhoea. Also vomiting, fatigue, lack of appetite.
Kennel cough	Contagious respiratory infection.	Combination of types of bacteria and virus. Most common: *Bordetella bronchiseptica* bacteria and parainfluenza virus.	Chronic cough.
Distemper	Disease primarily affecting respiratory and nervous system.	Virus that is related to the human measles virus.	Mild symptoms such as fever, lack of appetite and mucous secretion progress to evidence of brain damage, 'hard pad.'
Hepatitis	Virus primarily affecting the liver.	Canine adenovirus type I (CAV-1). Enters system when dog breathes in particles.	Lesser symptoms include listlessness, diarrhoea, vomiting. More severe symptoms include 'blue-eye' (clumps of virus in eye).
Coronavirus	Virus resulting in digestive problems.	Virus is spread through infected dog's faeces.	Stomach upset evidenced by lack of appetite, vomiting, diarrhoea.

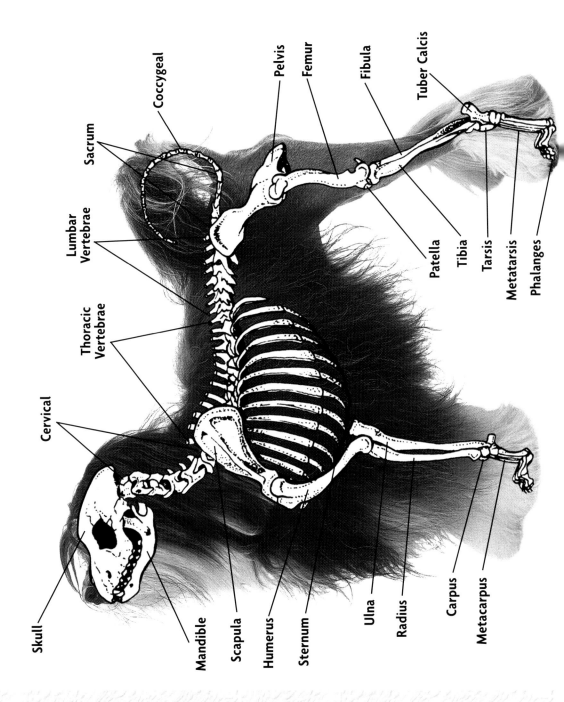

SKELETAL STRUCTURE OF THE LOWCHEN

Sophisticated health care and veterinary services can be very costly. It is not infrequent that important decisions are based upon financial considerations.

PREVENTATIVE MEDICINE

It is much easier, less costly and more effective to practise preventative medicine than to fight bouts of illness and disease. Properly bred puppies come from parents who were selected based upon their genetic disease profile. Their mothers should have been vaccinated, free of all internal and external parasites and properly nourished. For these reasons, a visit to the veterinary surgeon who cared for the dam is recommended. The dam can pass on disease resistance to her puppies, which can last for eight to ten weeks. She can also pass on parasites and many infections. That's why you should visit the veterinary surgeon who cared for the dam.

VACCINATION SCHEDULING

Most vaccinations are given by injection and should only be done

> ### BE CAREFUL WHERE YOU WALK YOUR DOG
> Dogs who have been exposed to lawns sprayed with herbicides have double and triple the rate of malignant lymphoma. Town dogs are especially at risk, as they are exposed to tailored lawns and gardens. Dogs perspire and absorb through their footpads. Be careful where your dog walks and always avoid any area that appears yellowed from chemical overspray.

by a veterinary surgeon. Both he and you should keep a record of the date of the injection, the identification of the vaccine and the amount given. Some vets give a first vaccination at eight weeks, but most dog breeders prefer the course not to commence until about ten weeks because of negating any antibodies passed on by the dam. The vaccination scheduling is usually based on a 15-day cycle. You must take your vet's advice regarding when to vaccinate as this may differ according to the vaccine used. Most vaccinations immunize your puppy against viruses.

The usual vaccines contain immunizing doses of several different viruses such as distemper, parvovirus, parainfluenza and hepatitis although some veterinary surgeons

> ### PROPER DIET
> Feeding your dog properly is very important. An incorrect diet could affect the dog's health, behaviour and nervous system, possibly making a normal dog into an aggressive one.

Normal hairs of a dog enlarged 200 times original size. The cuticle (outer covering) is clean and healthy. Unlike human hair that grows from the base, a dog's hair also grows from the end, as shown in the inset. Scanning electron micrographs by Dr Dennis Kunkel, University of Hawaii.

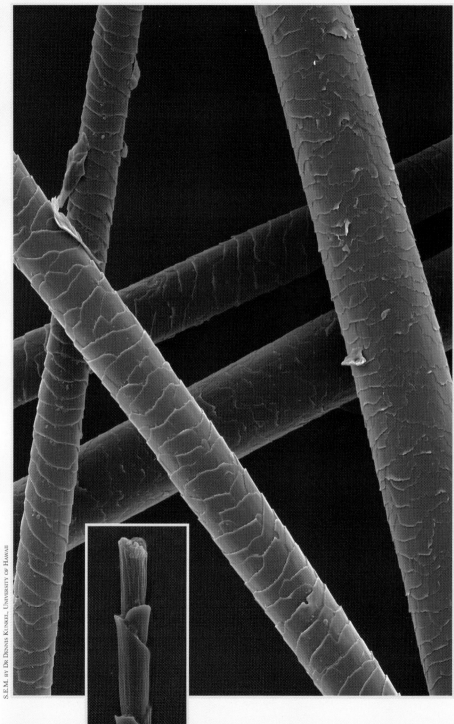

VACCINE ALLERGIES

Vaccines do not work all the time. Sometimes dogs are allergic to them and many times the antibodies, which are supposed to be stimulated by the vaccine, just are not produced. You should keep your dog in the veterinary clinic for an hour after it is vaccinated to be sure there are no allergic reactions.

puppy is at risk. You should rely upon professional advice. This is especially true for the booster-shot programme. Most vaccination programmes require a booster when the puppy is a year old and once a year thereafter. In some cases, circumstances may require more or less frequent immunizations. Kennel cough, more formally known as tracheobronchitis, is treated with a vaccine that is sprayed into the dog's nostrils. Kennel cough is usually included in routine vaccination, but this is often not so effective as for other major diseases.

recommend separate vaccines for each disease. There are other vaccines available when the

HEALTH AND VACCINATION SCHEDULE

AGE IN WEEKS:	6TH	8TH	10TH	12TH	14TH	16TH	20-24TH	1 YR
Worm Control	✔	✔	✔	✔	✔	✔	✔	
Neutering								✔
Heartworm*		✔		✔		✔	✔	
Parvovirus	✔		✔		✔		✔	✔
Distemper		✔		✔		✔		✔
Hepatitis		✔		✔		✔		✔
Leptospirosis								✔
Parainfluenza	✔		✔		✔			✔
Dental Examination		✔					✔	✔
Complete Physical		✔					✔	✔
Coronavirus				✔			✔	✔
Kennel Cough	✔							
Hip Dysplasia								✔
Rabies*							✔	

Vaccinations are not instantly effective. It takes about two weeks for the dog's immune system to develop antibodies. Most vaccinations require annual booster shots. Your veterinary surgeon should guide you in this regard.

*Not applicable in the United Kingdom

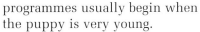

programmes usually begin when the puppy is very young.

The puppy will have its teeth examined and have its skeletal conformation and general health checked prior to certification by the veterinary surgeon. Puppies in certain breeds have problems with their kneecaps, cataracts and other eye problems, heart murmurs and undescended testicles. They may also have personality problems and your veterinary surgeon might have training in temperament evaluation.

MORE THAN VACCINES

Vaccinations help prevent your new puppy from contracting diseases, but they do not cure them. Proper nutrition as well as parasite control keep your dog healthy and less susceptible to many dangerous diseases. Remember that your dog depends on you to ensure his well-being.

WEANING TO FIVE MONTHS OLD

Puppies should be weaned by the time they are about two months old. A puppy that remains for at least eight weeks with its mother and littermates usually adapts better to other dogs and people later in its life.

Some new owners have their puppy examined by a veterinary surgeon immediately, which is a good idea. Vaccination

FIVE TO TWELVE MONTHS OF AGE

Unless you intend to breed or show your dog, neutering the puppy at six months of age is recommended. Discuss this with

'P' STANDS FOR PROBLEM

Urinary tract disease is a serious condition that requires immediate medical attention. Symptoms include urinating in inappropriate places or the need to urinate frequently in small amounts. Urinary tract disease is most effectively treated with antibiotics. To help promote good urinary tract health, owners must always be sure that a constant supply of fresh water is available to their pets.

KNOW WHEN TO POSTPONE A VACCINATION

While the visit to the vet is costly, it is never advisable to update a vaccination when visiting with a sick or pregnant dog. Vaccinations should be avoided for all elderly dogs. If your dog is showing the signs of any illness or any medical condition, no matter how serious or mild, including skin irritations, do not vaccinate. Likewise, a lame dog should never be vaccinated; any dog undergoing surgery or a dog on any immunosuppressant drugs should not be vaccinated until fully recovered.

your veterinary surgeon. Neutering has proven to be extremely beneficial to both male and female puppies. Besides eliminating the possibility of pregnancy, it inhibits (but does not prevent) breast cancer in bitches and prostate cancer in male dogs. Under no circumstances should a bitch be spayed prior to her first season.

Your veterinary surgeon should provide your puppy with a thorough dental evaluation at six months of age, ascertaining whether all the permanent teeth have erupted properly. A home dental care regimen should be initiated at six months, including brushing weekly and providing good dental devices (such as nylon bones). Regular dental care promotes healthy teeth, fresh breath and a longer life.

The Eyes Have It!

Eye disease is more prevalent among dogs than most people think, ranging from slight infections that are easily treated to serious complications that can lead to permanent sight loss. Eye diseases need veterinary attention in their early stages to prevent irreparable damage. This list provides descriptions of some common eye diseases:

Cataracts: Symptoms are white or grey discoloration of the eye lens and pupil, which causes fuzzy or completely obscured vision. Surgical treatment is required to remove the damaged lens and replace it with an artificial one.

Conjunctivitis: An inflammation of the mucous membrane that lines the eye socket, leaving the eyes red and puffy with excessive discharge. This condition is easily treated with antibiotics.

Corneal damage: The cornea is the transparent covering of the iris and pupil. Injuries are difficult to detect, but manifest themselves in surface abnormality, redness, pain and discharge. Most infections of the cornea are treated with antibiotics and require immediate medical attention.

Dry eye: This condition is caused by deficient production of tears that lubricate and protect the eye surface. A telltale sign is yellow-green discharge. Left undiagnosed, your dog will experience considerable pain, infections and possibly blindness. Dry eye is commonly treated with antibiotics, although more advanced cases may require surgery.

Glaucoma: This is caused by excessive fluid pressure in the eye. Symptoms are red eyes, grey or blue discoloration, pain, enlarged eyeballs and loss of vision. Antibiotics sometimes help, but surgery may be needed.

PARVO FOR THE COURSE

Canine parvovirus is a highly contagious disease that attacks puppies and older dogs. Spread through contact with infected faeces, parvovirus causes bloody diarrhoea, vomiting, heart damage, dehydration, shock and death. To prevent this tragedy, have your puppy begin his series of vaccinations at six to eight weeks. Be aware that the virus is easily spread and is carried on a dog's hair and feet, water bowls and other objects, as well as people's shoes and clothing.

ONE TO SEVEN YEARS

Once a year, your grown dog should visit the vet for an examination and vaccination boosters, if needed. Some vets recommend blood tests, thyroid level check and dental evaluation to accompany these annual visits. A thorough clinical evaluation by the vet can provide critical background information for your dog. Blood tests are often performed at one year of age, and dental examinations around the third or fourth birthday. In the long run, quality preventative care for your pet can save money, teeth and lives.

Don't Eat the Daisies!

Many plants and flowers are beautiful to look at, but can be highly toxic if ingested by your dog. Reactions range from abdominal pain and vomiting to convulsions and death. If the following plants are in your home, remove them. If they are outside your house or in your garden, avoid accidents by making sure your dog is never left unsupervised in those locations.

Azalea	Dumb cane	Mescal bean
Belladonna	Dutchman's breeches	Mushrooms
Bird of Paradise	Elephant's ear	Nightshade
Bulbs	Hydrangea	Philodendron
Calla lily	Jack-in-the-pulpit	Poinsettia
Cardinal flower	Jasmine	*Prunus* species
Castor bean	Jimsonweed	Tobacco
Chinaberry tree	Larkspur	Yellow jasmine
Daphne	Laurel	Yews, *Taxus* species
	Lily of the valley	

SKIN PROBLEMS IN LOWCHENS

Veterinary surgeons are consulted by dog owners for skin problems more than any other group of diseases or maladies. Dogs' skin is almost as sensitive as human skin and both suffer from almost the same ailments (though the occurrence of acne in dogs is rare!). For this reason, veterinary dermatology has developed into a speciality practised by many veterinary surgeons.

Since many skin problems have visual symptoms that are almost identical, it requires the skill of an experienced veterinary dermatologist to identify and cure many of the more severe skin disorders. Pet shops sell many treatments for skin problems but most of the treatments are directed at symptoms and not the underlying problem(s). If your dog is suffering from a skin disorder, you should seek professional assistance as quickly as possible. As with all diseases, the earlier a problem is identified and treated, the more successful is the cure.

PUPPY VACCINATIONS

Your veterinary surgeon will probably recommend that your puppy be vaccinated before you take him outside. There are airborne diseases, parasite eggs in the grass and unexpected visits from other dogs that might be dangerous to your puppy's health.

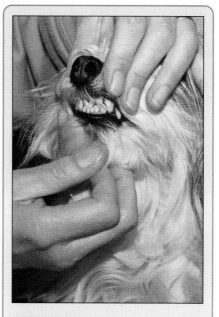

DENTAL HEALTH

A dental examination is in order when the dog is between six months and one year of age so any permanent teeth that have erupted incorrectly can be corrected. It is important to begin a brushing routine, preferably using a two-sided brushing technique, whereby both sides of the tooth are brushed at the same time. Durable nylon and safe edible chews should be a part of your puppy's arsenal for good health, good teeth and pleasant breath. The vast majority of dogs three to four years old and older have diseases of the gums from lack of dental attention. Using the various types of dental chews can be very effective in controlling dental plaque.

DID YOU KNOW?
Male dogs are neutered. The operation removes the testicles and requires that the dog be anaesthetised. Recovery takes about one week. Females are spayed. This is major surgery and it usually takes a bitch two weeks to recover.

Hereditary Skin Disorders

Veterinary dermatologists are currently researching a number of skin disorders that are believed to have an hereditary basis. These inherited diseases are transmitted by both parents, who appear (phenotypically) normal but have a recessive gene for the disease, meaning that they carry, but are not affected by, the disease. These diseases pose serious problems to breeders because in some instances there is no method of identifying carriers. Often the secondary diseases associated with these skin conditions are even more debilitating than the disorder itself, including cancers and respiratory problems; others

Vitamins Recommended for Dogs

Some breeders and vets recommend the supplementation of vitamins to a dog's diet—others do not. Before embarking on a vitamin programme, consult your vet.

Vitamin / Dosage	Food source	Benefits
A / 10,000 IU/week	Eggs, butter, yoghurt, meat	Skin, eyes, hind legs, haircoat
B / Varies	Organs, cottage cheese, sardines	Appetite, fleas, heart, skin and coat
C / 2000 mg+	Fruit, legumes, leafy green vegetables	Healing, arthritis, kidneys
D / Varies	Cod liver, cheese, organs, eggs	Bones, teeth, endocrine system
E / 250 IU daily	Leafy green vegetables, meat, wheat germ oil	Skin, muscles, nerves, healing, digestion
F / Varies	Fish oils, raw meat	Heart, skin, coat, fleas
K / Varies	Naturally in body, not through food	Blood clotting

can be lethal.

Among the hereditary skin disorders, for which the mode of inheritance is known, are: acrodermatitis, cutaneous asthenia (Ehlers-Danlos syndrome), sebaceous adenitis, cyclic hematopoiesis, dermatomyositis, IgA deficiency, colour dilution alopecia and nodular dermatofibrosis. Some of these disorders are limited to one or two breeds and others affect a large number of breeds. All inherited diseases must be diagnosed and treated by a veterinary specialist.

A SKUNKY PROBLEM

Have you noticed your dog dragging his rump along the floor? If so, it is likely that his anal sacs are impacted or possibly infected. The anal sacs are small pouches located on both sides of the anus under the skin and muscles. They are about the size and shape of a grape and contain a foul-smelling liquid. Their contents are usually emptied when the dog has a bowel movement, but if they are not emptied completely, they will impact, which will cause your dog a lot of pain. Fortunately, your veterinary surgeon can tend to this problem easily by draining the sacs for the dog. Be aware that your dog might also empty his anal sacs in cases of extreme fright.

MANY KINDS OF EARS

Not every dog's ears are the same. Ears that are open to the air are healthier than ears with poor air circulation. Sometimes a dog can have two differently shaped ears. You should not probe inside your dog's ears as shown above. Only clean that which is accessible with a soft cotton wipe.

PARASITE BITES

Many of us are allergic to insect bites. The bites itch, erupt and may even become infected. Dogs have the same reaction to fleas, ticks and/or mites. When an insect lands on you, you have the chance to whisk it away with your hand. Unfortunately, when your dog is bitten by a flea, tick or mite, it can only scratch it away or bite it. By the time the dog has been bitten, the parasite has done some of its damage. It may also have laid eggs to cause further problems in the near future. The itching from parasite bites is probably due to the saliva injected into the site when the parasite sucks the dog's blood.

Auto-Immune Skin Conditions

Auto-immune skin conditions are commonly referred to as being allergic to yourself, while allergies are usually inflammatory reactions to an outside stimulus. Auto-immune diseases cause serious damage to the tissues that

PET ADVANTAGES

If you do not intend to show or breed your new puppy, your veterinary surgeon will probably recommend that you spay your female or neuter your male. Some people believe neutering leads to weight gain, but if you feed and exercise your dog properly, this is easily avoided. Spaying or neutering can actually have many positive outcomes, such as:
• training becomes easier, as the dog focuses less on the urge to mate and more on you!
• females are protected from unplanned pregnancy as well as ovarian and uterine cancers.
• males are guarded from testicular tumours and have a reduced risk of developing prostate cancer.
  Talk to your vet regarding the right age to spay/neuter and other aspects of the procedure.

'HEALTH PASSPORT'

It was announced in April 1999 that the severe quarantine laws imposed on animals entering Britain from other rabies-free countries would become a thing of the past by April 2001. Rather than being confined to a kennel for six months upon arrival in Britain, animals undergo a series of blood tests and vaccinations, and are identifed by microchip implantation. Qualified pets receive a 'health passport' that allows their owners to travel with them in between Britain and other (mostly European) countries in which rabies does not exist.

  Animals from countries such as the United States and Canada, where rabies is a problem, still will be subject to quarantine. Although veterinary standards are high in these countries, recently infected dogs may test negative to the disease and, without the quarantine period, may unknowingly introduce rabies into previously unaffected countries.

are involved.

  The best known auto-immune disease is lupus, which affects people as well as dogs. The symptoms are variable and may affect the kidneys, bones, blood chemistry and skin. It can be fatal

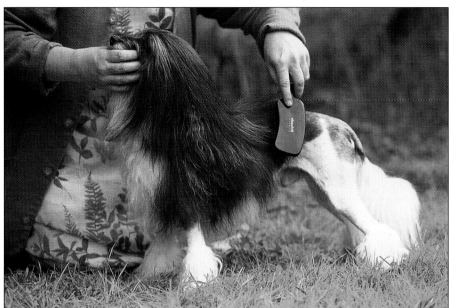

Do not neglect the Lowchen's beautiful coat. An owner who spends time grooming his Lowchen daily can enjoy the dog's luxuriant coat as well as discover any abnormalities that can appear on the dog's skin.

to both dogs and humans, though it is not thought to be transmissible. It is usually successfully treated with cortisone, prednisone or a similar corticosteroid, but extensive use of these drugs can have harmful side effects.

Skin Allergies

Skin allergies do not frequently occur in the Lowchen, but in the odd cases in which they do, they can often be kept under control with a carefully considered diet. The allergy may be noticed as 'hot spots' on the skin, despite no signs of external parasites. A low-protein diet often seems to suit skin troubles.

It is often extremely difficult to ascertain the cause of a skin allergy. There are many possibilities, ranging from the sitting room carpet, the shampoo used when bathing and, quite frequently, certain grasses and moulds. In case of a skin allergy, it is a good idea to change shampoo, conditioning rinse and any other coat sprays used, for these are perhaps the easiest items to eliminate before looking further if necessary.

Airborne Allergies

Another interesting allergy is pollen allergy. Humans have hay fever, rose fever and other fevers with which they suffer during the pollinating season. Many dogs suffer the same allergies. When the pollen count is high, your dog

CUSHING'S DISEASE
Cases of hyperactive adrenal glands (Cushing's disease) have been traced to the drinking of highly chlorinated water. Aerate or age your dog's drinking water before offering it.

might suffer but don't expect him to sneeze and have a runny nose like humans. Dogs react to pollen allergies the same way they react to fleas—they scratch and bite themselves.

Dogs, like humans, can be tested for allergens. Discuss the testing with your veterinary dermatologist.

FOOD PROBLEMS

FOOD ALLERGIES
Dogs are allergic to many foods that are best-sellers and highly recommended by breeders and veterinary surgeons. Changing the brand of food that you buy may not eliminate the problem if the element to which the dog is allergic is contained in the new brand.

Recognising a food allergy is difficult. Humans vomit or have rashes when they eat a food to which they are allergic. Dogs neither vomit nor (usually) develop a rash. They react in the same manner as they do to an airborne or flea allergy; they itch, scratch and bite, thus making the diagnosis extremely difficult. While pollen allergies and parasite bites are usually seasonal, food allergies are year-round problems.

FOOD INTOLERANCE
Food intolerance is the inability of the dog to completely digest certain foods. Puppies that may have done very well on their mother's milk may not do well on cow's milk. The result of this food intolerance may be loose bowels, passing gas and stomach pains. These are the only obvious symptoms of food intolerance and that makes diagnosis difficult.

TREATING FOOD PROBLEMS
It is possible to handle food allergies and food intolerance yourself. Put your dog on a diet that it has never had. Obviously if it has never eaten this new food it can't have been allergic or intolerant of it. Start with a single ingredient that is not in the dog's diet at the present time.

FACT OR FICTION?
The myth that dogs need extra fat in their diets can be harmful. Should your vet recommend extra fat, use safflower oil instead of animal oils. Safflower oil has been shown to be less likely to cause allergic reactions.

Ingredients like chopped beef or fish are common in dogs' diets, so try something more exotic like rabbit, pheasant or even just vegetables. Keep the dog on this diet (with no additives) for a month. If the symptoms of food allergy or intolerance disappear,

THE SAME ALLERGIES
Chances are that you and your dog will have the same allergies. Your allergies are readily recognisable and usually easily treated. Your dog's allergies may be masked.

Puppies and adults alike can develop food allergies. Consult a dietary expert if you suspect that your pup is suffering from a food allergy.

chances are your dog has a food allergy.

Don't think that the single ingredient cured the problem. You still must find a suitable diet and ascertain which ingredient in the old diet was objectionable. This is most easily done by

DID YOU KNOW?
Your dog's protein needs are changeable. High activity level, stress, climate and other physical factors may require your dog to have more protein in his diet. Check with your veterinary surgeon.

adding ingredients to the new diet one at a time. Let the dog stay on the modified diet for a month before you add another ingredient. Eventually, you will determine the ingredient that caused the adverse reaction.

An alternative method is to carefully study the ingredients in the diet to which your dog is allergic or intolerant. Identify the main ingredient in this diet and eliminate the main ingredient by buying a different food that does not have that ingredient. Keep experimenting until the symptoms disappear after one month on the new diet.

EXTERNAL PARASITES

FLEAS

Of all the problems to which dogs are prone, none is more well known and frustrating than fleas. Flea infestation is relatively simple to cure but difficult to prevent. Parasites that are harboured inside the body are a bit more difficult to eradicate but they are easier to control.

To control flea infestation, you have to understand the flea's life cycle. Fleas are often thought of as a summertime problem, but centrally heated homes have changed the patterns and fleas can be found at any time of the year. The most effective method of flea control is a two-stage approach: one stage to kill the adult fleas, and the other to control the development of pre-adult fleas. Unfortunately, no single active ingredient is effective against all stages of the life cycle.

LIFE CYCLE STAGES

During its life, a flea will pass through four life stages: egg, larva, pupa and adult. The adult stage is the most visible and irritating stage of the flea life cycle, and this is why the majority of flea-control products concentrate on this stage.

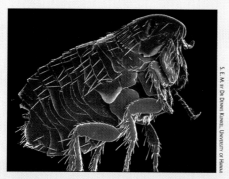

A scanning electron micrograph (S. E. M.) of a dog flea, *Ctenocephalides canis.*

S. E. M. BY DR DENNIS KUNKEL, UNIVERSITY OF HAWAII

Magnified head of a dog flea, *Ctenocephalides canis.*

S. E. M. BY DR DENNIS KUNKEL, UNIVERSITY OF HAWAII

A Look at Fleas

Fleas have been around for millions of years and have adapted to changing host animals. They are able to go through a complete life cycle in less than one month or they can extend their lives to almost two years by remaining as pupae or cocoons. They do not need blood or any other food for up to 20 months.

They have been measured as being able to jump 300,000 times and can jump 150 times their length in any direction including straight up. Those are just a few of the reasons why they are so successful in infesting a dog!

The fact is that adult fleas account for only 1% of the total flea population, and the other 99% exist in pre-adult stages, i.e. eggs, larvae and pupae. The pre-adult stages are barely visible to the naked eye.

THE LIFE CYCLE OF THE FLEA

Eggs are laid on the dog, usually in quantities of about 20 or 30, several times a day. The female adult flea must have a blood meal before each egg-laying session. When first laid, the eggs will cling to the dog's fur, as the eggs are still moist. However, they will quickly dry out and fall from the dog, especially if the dog moves around or scratches. Many eggs will fall off in the dog's favourite area or an area in which he spends a lot of time, such as his bed.

Once the eggs fall from the dog onto the carpet or furniture, they will hatch into larvae. This takes from one to ten days. Larvae are not particularly mobile, and will usually travel only a few inches from where they hatch. However, they do have a tendency to move away from light and heavy traffic—under furniture and behind doors are common places to find high quantities of flea larvae.

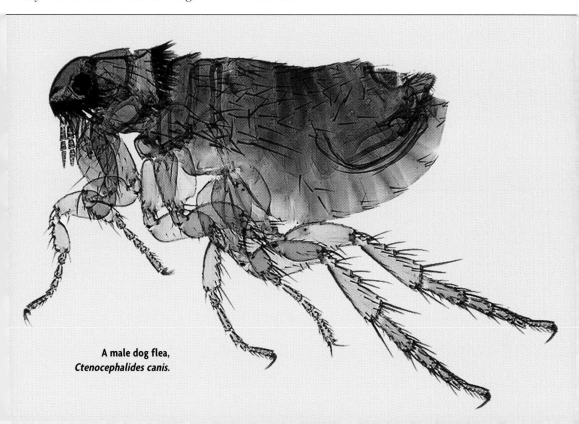

**A male dog flea,
Ctenocephalides canis.**

The flea larvae feed on dead organic matter, including adult flea faeces, until they are ready to change into adult fleas. Fleas will usually remain as larvae for around seven days. After this period, the larvae will pupate into protective pupae. While inside the pupae, the larvae will undergo metamorphosis and change into adult fleas. This can take as little time as a few days, but the adult fleas can remain inside the pupae waiting to hatch for up to two years. The pupae are signalled to hatch by certain stimuli, such as physical pressure—the pupae's being stepped on, heat from an animal lying on the pupae or increased carbon dioxide levels and vibrations—indicating that a suitable host is available.

Once hatched, the adult flea must feed within a few days. Once the adult flea finds a host, it will not leave voluntarily. It only becomes dislodged by grooming or the host animal's scratching. The adult flea will remain on the host for the duration of its life unless forcibly removed.

DID YOU KNOW?
Never mix flea control products without first consulting your veterinary surgeon. Some products can become toxic when combined with others and can cause serious or fatal consequences.

DID YOU KNOW?
Flea-killers are poisonous. You should not spray these toxic chemicals on areas of a dog's body that he licks, on his genitals or on his face. Flea killers taken internally are a better answer, but check with your vet in case internal therapy is not advised for your dog.

TREATING THE ENVIRONMENT AND THE DOG
Treating fleas should be a two-pronged attack. First, the environment needs to be treated; this includes carpets and furniture, especially the dog's bedding and areas underneath furniture. The environment should be treated with a household spray containing an Insect Growth Regulator (IGR) and an insecticide to kill the adult fleas. Most IGRs are effective against eggs and larvae; they actually mimic the fleas' own hormones and stop the eggs and larvae from developing into adult fleas. There are currently no treatments available to attack the pupa stage of the life cycle, so the adult insecticide is used to kill the newly hatched adult fleas before they find a host. Most IGRs are active for many months, whilst adult insecticides are only active for a few days.

When treating with a household spray, it is a good idea to vacuum before applying the product. This stimulates as many

Opposite page: A scanning electron micrograph of a dog or cat flea, *Ctenocephalides*, magnified more than 100x. This image has been colorized for effect.

The Life Cycle of the Flea

Eggs

Larva

Pupa

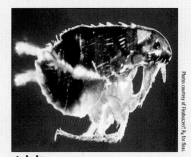

Adult

Photos courtesy of Fleabusters® Rx for fleas.

Flea Control

IGR (INSECT GROWTH REGULATOR)

Two types of products should be used when treating fleas—a product to treat the pet and a product to treat the home. Adult fleas represent less than 1% of the flea population. The pre-adult fleas (eggs, larvae and pupae) represent more than 99% of the flea population and are found in the environment; it is in the case of pre-adult fleas that products containing an Insect Growth Regulator (IGR) should be used in the home.

IGRs are a new class of compounds used to prevent the development of insects. They do not kill the insect outright, but instead use the insect's biology against it to stop it from completing its growth. Products that contain methoprene are the world's first and leading IGRs. Used to control fleas and other insects, this type of IGR will stop flea larvae from developing and protect the house for up to seven months.

EN GARDE:
CATCHING FLEAS OFF GUARD!

Consider the following ways to arm yourself against fleas:

• Add a small amount of pennyroyal or eucalyptus oil to your dog's bath. These natural remedies repel fleas.

• Supplement your dog's food with fresh garlic (minced or grated) and a hearty amount of brewer's yeast, both of which ward off fleas.

• Use a flea comb on your dog daily. Submerge fleas in a cup of bleach to kill them quickly.

• Confine the dog to only a few rooms to limit the spread of fleas in the home.

• Vacuum daily...and get all of the crevices! Dispose of the bag every few days until the problem is under control.

• Wash your dog's bedding daily. Cover cushions where your dog sleeps with towels, and wash the towels often.

pupae as possible to hatch into adult fleas. The vacuum cleaner should also be treated with a flea treatment to prevent the eggs and larvae that have been hoovered into the vacuum bag from hatching.

The second stage of treatment is to apply an adult insecticide to the dog. Traditionally, this would be in the form of a collar or a spray, but more recent innovations include digestible insecticides that poison the fleas when they ingest the dog's blood. Alternatively, there are drops that, when placed on the back of the animal's neck, spread throughout the fur and skin to kill adult fleas.

Photo by Dwight R Kuhn

Dwight R Kuhn's magnificent action photo showing a flea jumping from a dog's back.

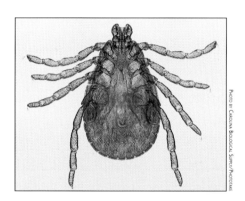

Photo by Carolina Biological Supply/Phototake

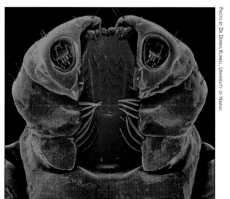

Photo by Dr Dennis Kunkel, University of Hawaii

TICKS AND MITES

Though not as common as fleas, ticks and mites are found all over the tropical and temperate world. They don't bite, like fleas; they harpoon. They dig their sharp proboscis (nose) into the dog's skin and drink the blood. Their only food and drink is dog's blood. Dogs can get Lyme disease, Rocky Mountain spotted fever (normally found in the US only), paralysis and many other diseases from ticks and mites. They may live where fleas are found and they like to hide in cracks or seams in walls wherever dogs live. They are controlled the same way fleas

A brown dog tick, *Rhipicephalus sanguineus*, is an uncommon but annoying tick found on dogs.

The head of a dog tick, *Dermacentor variabilis*, enlarged and coloured for effect.

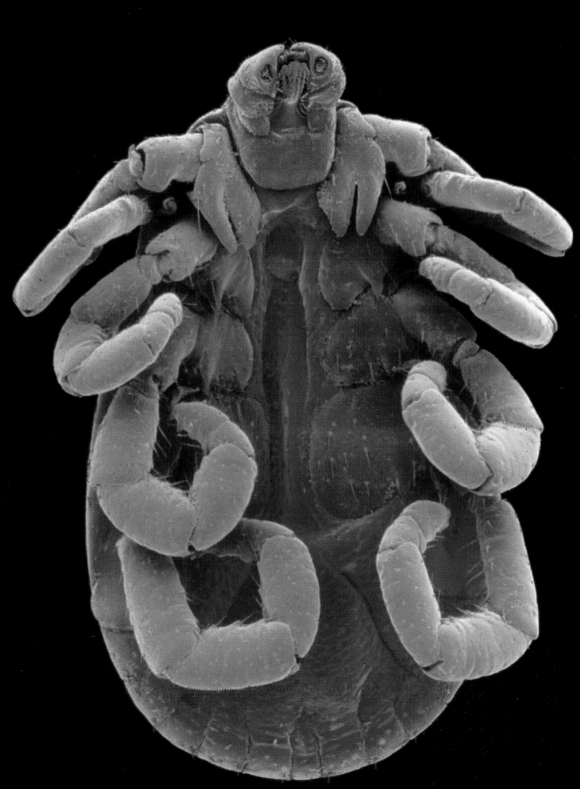

are controlled.

The dog tick, *Dermacentor variabilis*, may well be the most common dog tick in many geographical areas, especially those areas where the climate is hot and humid.

Most dog ticks have life expectancies of a week to six months, depending upon climatic conditions. They can neither jump nor fly, but they can crawl slowly and can range up to 5 metres (16 feet) to reach a sleeping or unsuspecting dog.

BEWARE THE DEER TICK

The great outdoors may be fun for your dog, but it also is a home to dangerous ticks. Deer ticks carry a bacterium known as *Borrelia burgdorferi* and are most active in the autumn and spring. When infections are caught early, penicillin and tetracycline are effective antibiotics, but if left untreated the bacteria may cause neurological, kidney and cardiac problems as well as long-term trouble with walking and painful joints.

Opposite page: The dog tick, *Dermacentor variabilis*, is probably the most common tick found on dogs. Look at the strength in its eight legs! No wonder it's hard to detach them.

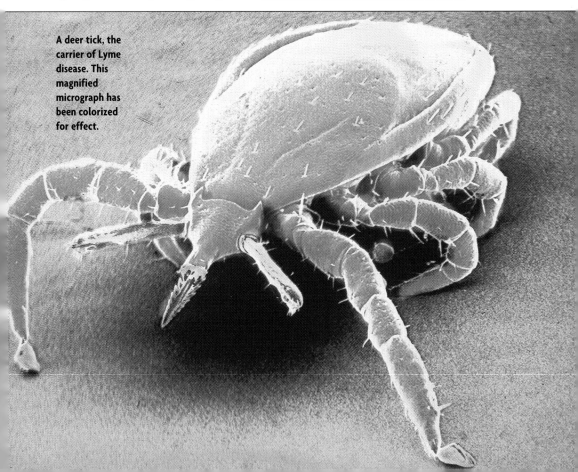

A deer tick, the carrier of Lyme disease. This magnified micrograph has been colorized for effect.

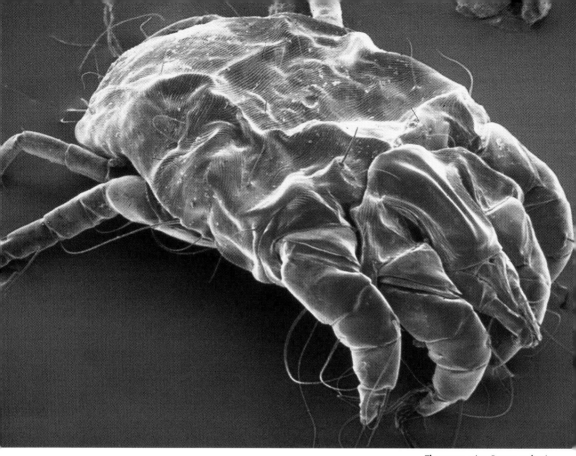

The mange mite, *Psoroptes bovis.*

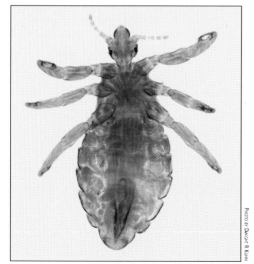

Human lice look like dog lice; the two are closely related.

MANGE

Mites cause a skin irritation called mange. Some are contagious, like *Cheyletiella*, ear mites, scabies and chiggers. Mites that cause ear-mite infestations are usually controlled with Lindane, which can only be administered by a vet, followed by Tresaderm at home.

It is essential that your dog be treated for mange as quickly as possible because some forms of mange are transmissible to people.

INTERNAL PARASITES

Most animals—fishes, birds and mammals, including dogs and humans—have worms and other parasites that live inside their bodies. According to Dr Herbert R Axelrod, the fish pathologist, there are two kinds of parasites: dumb and smart. The smart parasites live in peaceful cooperation with their hosts (symbiosis), while the dumb parasites kill their hosts. Most of the worm infections are relatively easy to control. If they are not controlled, they weaken the host dog to the point that other medical problems occur, but they are not dumb parasites.

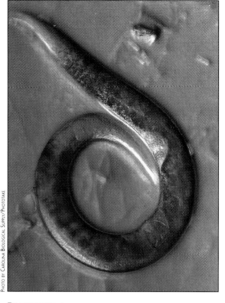

PHOTO BY CAROLINA BIOLOGICAL SUPPLY/PHOTOTAKE

The roundworm, *Rhabditis.* The roundworm can infect both dogs and humans.

ROUNDWORM

Average size dogs can pass 1,360,000 roundworm eggs every day.

For example, if there were only 1 million dogs in the world, the world would be saturated with 1,300 metric tonnes of dog faeces.

These faeces would contain 15,000,000,000 roundworm eggs.

It's known that 7–31% of home gardens and children's play boxes in the US contain roundworm eggs.

Flushing dog's faeces down the toilet is not a safe practice because the usual sewage treatments do not destroy roundworm eggs.

Infected puppies start shedding roundworm eggs at 3 weeks of age. They can be infected by their mother's milk.

ROUNDWORMS

The roundworms that infect dogs are scientifically known as *Toxocara canis*. They live in the dog's intestines. The worms shed eggs continually. It has been estimated that a dog produces about 150 grammes of faeces every day. Each gramme of faeces averages 10,000–12,000 eggs of roundworms. There are no known areas in which dogs roam that do not contain roundworm eggs. The greatest danger of roundworms is that they infect people too! It is wise to have your dog tested regularly for roundworms.

Pigs also have roundworm infections that can be passed to humans and dogs. The typical roundworm parasite is called *Ascaris lumbricoides*.

DEWORMING

Ridding your puppy of worms is VERY IMPORTANT because certain worms that puppies carry, such as tapeworms and roundworms, can infect humans.

Breeders initiate a deworming programme at or about four weeks of age. The routine is repeated every two or three weeks until the puppy is three months old. The breeder from whom you obtained your puppy should provide you with the complete details of the deworming programme.

Your veterinary surgeon can prescribe and monitor the programme of deworming for you. The usual programme is treating the puppy every 15–20 days until the puppy is positively worm-free.

It is advised that you only treat your puppy with drugs that are recommended professionally.

HOOKWORMS

The worm *Ancylostoma caninum* is commonly called the dog hookworm. It is also dangerous to humans and cats. It has teeth by which it attaches itself to the intestines of the dog. It changes the site of its attachment about six times a day and the dog loses blood from each detachment, possibly causing iron-deficiency anaemia. Hookworms are easily purged from the dog with many medications. Milbemycin oxime, which also serves as a heartworm preventative in Collies, can be used for this purpose.

In Britain the 'temperate climate' hookworm (*Uncinaria stenocephala*) is rarely found in pet or show dogs, but can occur in hunting packs, racing Greyhounds and sheepdogs because the worms can be prevalent wherever dogs are exercised regularly on grassland.

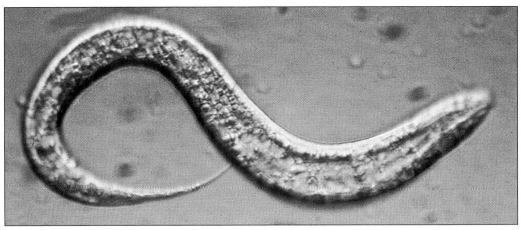

The infective stage of the hookworm larva.

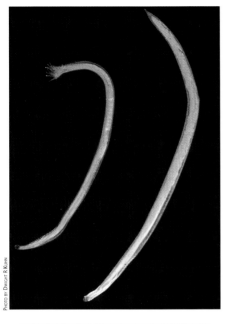

PHOTO BY DWIGHT R KUHN

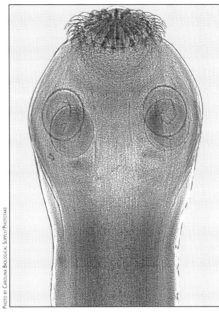

PHOTO BY CAROLINA BIOLOGICAL SUPPLY/PHOTOTAKE

Left:
Male and female hookworms, *Ancylostoma caninum*, are uncommonly found in pet or show dogs in Britain. Hookworms may infect other dogs that have exposure to grasslands.

Right:
The head and rostellum (the round prominence on the scolex) of a tapeworm, which infects dogs and humans.

TAPEWORM

Humans, rats, squirrels, foxes, coyotes, wolves, mixed breeds of dogs and purebred dogs are all susceptible to tapeworm infection. Except in humans, tapeworm is usually not a fatal infection.

Infected individuals can harbour a thousand parasitic worms.

Tapeworms have two sexes—male and female (many other worms have only one sex—male and female in the same worm).

If dogs eat infected rats or mice, they get the tapeworm disease.

One month after attaching to a dog's intestine, the worm starts shedding eggs. These eggs are infective immediately.

Infective eggs can live for a few months without a host animal.

TAPEWORMS

There are many species of tapeworm. They are carried by fleas! The dog eats the flea and starts the tapeworm cycle. Humans can also be infected with tapeworms, so don't eat fleas! Fleas are so small that your dog could pass them onto your hands, your plate or your food and thus make it possible for you to ingest a flea that is carrying tapeworm eggs.

While tapeworm infection is not life-threatening in dogs (smart parasite!), it can be the cause of a very serious liver disease for humans. About 50 percent of the humans infected with *Echinococcus multilocularis*, a type of tapeworm that causes alveolar hydatis, perish.

HEARTWORMS

Heartworms are thin, extended worms up to 30 cms (12 ins) long, which live in a dog's heart and the major blood vessels surrounding it. Dogs may have up to 200 worms. Symptoms may be loss of energy, loss of appetite, coughing, the development of a pot belly and anaemia.

Heartworms are transmitted by mosquitoes. The mosquito drinks the blood of an infected dog and takes in larvae with the blood. The larvae, called microfilaria, develop within the body of the mosquito and are passed on to the next dog bitten after the larvae mature. It takes two to three weeks for the larvae to develop to the infective stage within the body of the mosquito. Dogs should be treated at about six weeks of age, and maintained on a prophylactic dose given monthly.

Blood testing for heartworms is not necessarily indicative of how seriously your dog is infected. This is a dangerous disease. Although heartworm is a problem for dogs in America, Australia, Asia and Central Europe, dogs in the United Kingdom are not currently affected by heartworm.

The heart of a dog infected with canine heartworm, *Dirofilaria immitis.*

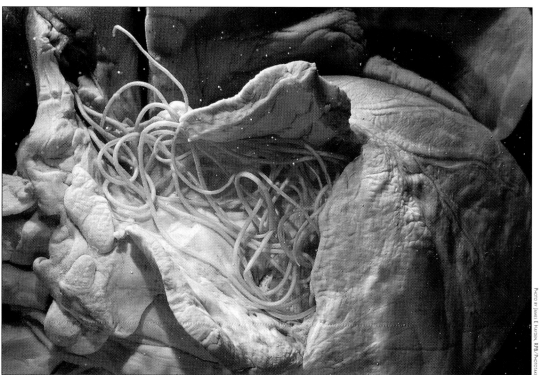

First Aid at a Glance

Burns
Place the affected area under cool water; use ice if only a small area is burnt.

Bee/Insect bites
Apply ice to relieve swelling; antihistamine dosed properly.

Animal bites
Clean any bleeding area; apply pressure until bleeding subsides; go to the vet.

Spider bites
Use cold compress and a pressurised pack to inhibit venom's spreading.

Antifreeze poisoning
Induce vomiting with hydrogen peroxide. Seek *immediate* veterinary help!

Fish hooks
Removal best handled by vet; hook must be cut in order to remove.

Snake bites
Pack ice around bite; contact vet quickly; identify snake for proper antivenin.

Car accident
Move dog from roadway with blanket; seek veterinary aid.

Shock
Calm the dog, keep him warm; seek immediate veterinary help.

Nosebleed
Apply cold compress to the nose; apply pressure to any visible abrasion.

Bleeding
Apply pressure above the area; treat wound by applying a cotton pack.

Heat stroke
Submerge dog in cold bath; cool down with fresh air and water; go to the vet.

Frostbite/Hypothermia
Warm the dog with a warm bath, electric blankets or hot water bottles.

Abrasions
Clean the wound and wash out thoroughly with fresh water; apply antiseptic.

 Remember: an injured dog may attempt to bite a helping hand from fear and confusion. Always muzzle the dog before trying to offer assistance.

HOMEOPATHY:
an alternative
to conventional
medicine

'Less is Most'

Using this principle, the strength of a homeopathic remedy is measured by the number of serial dilutions that were undertaken to create it. The greater the number of serial dilutions, the greater the strength of the homeopathic remedy. The potency of a remedy that has been made by making a dilution of 1 part in 100 parts (or 1/100) is 1c or 1cH. If this remedy is subjected to a series of further dilutions, each one being 1/100, a more dilute and stronger remedy is produced. If the remedy is diluted in this way six times, it is called 6c or 6cH. A dilution of 6c is 1 part in 1,000,000,000,000. In general, higher potencies in more frequent doses are better for acute symptoms and lower potencies in more infrequent doses are more useful for chronic, long-standing problems.

CURING OUR DOGS NATURALLY

Holistic medicine means treating the whole animal as a unique, perfect living being. Generally, holistic treatments do not suppress the symptoms that the body naturally produces, as do most medications prescribed by conventional doctors and vets. Holistic methods seek to cure disease by regaining balance and harmony in the patient's environment. Some of these methods include use of nutritional therapy, herbs, flower essences, aromatherapy, acupuncture, massage, chiropractic and, of course the most popular holistic approach, homeopathy. Homeopathy is a theory or system of treating illness with small doses of substances which, if administered in larger quantities, would produce the symptoms that the patient already has. This approach is often described as 'like cures like.' Although modern veterinary medicine is geared toward the 'quick fix,' homeopathy relies on the belief that, given the time, the body is able to heal itself and return to its natural, healthy state.

Choosing a remedy to cure a problem in our dogs is the difficult part of homeopathy. Consult with your veterinary surgeon for a professional diagnosis of your dog's symptoms. Often these symptoms require immediate conventional care. If your vet is willing, and knowledgeable, you may attempt a homeopathic remedy. Be aware that cortisone prevents homeopathic remedies from working. There are hundreds of possibilities and combinations to cure many problems in dogs, from basic physical problems such as excessive moulting, fleas or other parasites, unattractive doggy odour, bad breath, upset tummy, dry, oily or dull coat, diarrhoea, ear problems or eye discharge (including tears and dry or mucousy matter), to behavioural abnormalities, such as fear of loud noises, habitual licking, poor appetite, excessive barking, obesity and various phobias. From alumina to zincum metallicum, the remedies span the planet and the imagination…from flowers and weeds to chemicals, insect droppings, diesel smoke and volcanic ash.

Using 'Like to Treat Like'

Unlike conventional medicines that suppress symptoms, homeopathic remedies treat illnesses with small doses of substances that, if administered in larger quantities, would produce the symptoms that the patient already has. Whilst the same homeopathic remedy can be used to treat different symptoms in different dogs, here are some interesting remedies and their uses.

Apis Mellifica
(made from honey bee venom) can be used for allergies or to reduce swelling that occurs in acutely infected kidneys.

Diesel Smoke
can be used to help control travel sickness.

Calcarea Fluorica
(made from calcium fluoride which helps harden bone structure) can be useful in treating hard lumps in tissues.

Natrum Muriaticum
(made from common salt, sodium chloride) is useful in treating thin, thirsty dogs.

Nitricum Acidum
(made from nitric acid) is used for symptoms you would expect to see from contact with acids such as lesions, especially where the skin joins the linings of body orifices or openings such as the lips and nostrils.

Symphytum
(made from the herb Knitbone, *Symphytum officianale*) is used to encourage bones to heal.

Urtica Urens
(made from the common stinging nettle) is used in treating painful, irritating rashes.

HOMEOPATHIC REMEDIES FOR YOUR DOG

Symptom/Ailment	Possible Remedy
ALLERGIES	Apis Mellifica 30c, Astacus Fluviatilis 6c, Pulsatilla 30c, Urtica Urens 6c
ALOPECIA	Alumina 30c, Lycopodium 30c, Sepia 30c, Thallium 6c
ANAL GLANDS (BLOCKED)	Hepar Sulphuris Calcareum 30c, Sanicula 6c, Silicea 6c
ARTHRITIS	Rhus Toxicodendron 6c, Bryonia Alba 6c
CATARACT	Calcarea Carbonica 6c, Conium Maculatum 6c, Phosphorus 30c, Silicea 30c
CONSTIPATION	Alumina 6c, Carbo Vegetabilis 30c, Graphites 6c, Nitricum Acidum 30c, Silicea 6c
COUGHING	Aconitum Napellus 6c, Belladonna 30c, Hyoscyamus Niger 30c, Phosphorus 30c
DIARRHOEA	Arsenicum Album 30c, Aconitum Napellus 6c, Chamomilla 30c, Mercurius Corrosivus 30c
DRY EYE	Zincum Metallicum 30c
EAR PROBLEMS	Aconitum Napellus 30c, Belladonna 30c, Hepar Sulphuris 30c, Tellurium 30c, Psorinum 200c
EYE PROBLEMS	Borax 6c, Aconitum Napellus 30c, Graphites 6c, Staphysagria 6c, Thuja Occidentalis 30c
GLAUCOMA	Aconitum Napellus 30c, Apis Mellifica 6c, Phosphorus 30c
HEAT STROKE	Belladonna 30c, Gelsemium Sempervirens 30c, Sulphur 30c
HICCOUGHS	Cinchona Deficinalis 6c
HIP DYSPLASIA	Colocynthis 6c, Rhus Toxicodendron 6c, Bryonia Alba 6c
INCONTINENCE	Argentum Nitricum 6c, Causticum 30c, Conium Maculatum 30c, Pulsatilla 30c, Sepia 30c
INSECT BITES	Apis Mellifica 30c, Cantharis 30c, Hypericum Perforatum 6c, Urtica Urens 30c
ITCHING	Alumina 30c, Arsenicum Album 30c, Carbo Vegetabilis 30c, Hypericum Perforatum 6c, Mezerium 6c, Sulphur 30c
KENNEL COUGH	Drosera 6c, Ipecacuanha 30c
MASTITIS	Apis Mellifica 30c, Belladonna 30c, Urtica Urens 1m
PATELLAR LUXATION	Gelsemium Sempervirens 6c, Rhus Toxicodendron 6c
PENIS PROBLEMS	Aconitum Napellus 30c, Hepar Sulphuris Calcareum 30c, Pulsatilla 30c, Thuja Occidentalis 6c
PUPPY TEETHING	Calcarea Carbonica 6c, Chamomilla 6c, Phytolacca 6c
TRAVEL SICKNESS	Cocculus 6c, Petroleum 6c

Recognising a Sick Dog

Unlike colicky babies and cranky children, our canine kids cannot tell us when they are feeling ill. Therefore, there are a number of signs that owners can identify to know that their dogs are not feeling well.

Take note for physical manifestations such as:

- unusual, bad odour, including bad breath
- excessive moulting
- wax in the ears, chronic ear irritation
- oily, flaky, dull haircoat
- mucous, tearing or similar discharge in the eyes
- fleas or mites
- mucous in stool, diarrhoea
- sensitivity to petting or handling
- licking at paws, scratching face, etc.

Keep an eye out for behavioural changes as well including:

- lethargy, idleness
- lack of patience or general irritability
- lack of appetite, digestive problems
- phobias (fear of people, loud noises, etc.)
- strange behaviour, suspicion, fear
- coprophagia
- more frequent barking
- whimpering, crying

Get Well Soon

You don't need a DVR or a BVMA to provide good TLC to your sick or recovering dog, but you do need to pay attention to some details that normally wouldn't bother him. The following tips will aid Fido's recovery and get him back on his paws again:

- Keep his space free of irritating smells, like heavy perfumes and air fresheners.
- Rest is the best medicine! Avoid harsh lighting that will prevent your dog from sleeping. Shade him from bright sunlight during the day and dim the lights in the evening.
- Keep the noise level down. Animals are more sensitive to sound when they are sick.

- Be attentive to any necessary temperature adjustments. A dog with a fever needs a cool room and cold liquids. A bitch that is whelping or recovering from surgery will be more comfortable in a warm room, consuming warm liquids and food.
- You wouldn't send a sick child back to school early, so don't rush your dog back into a full routine until he seems absolutely ready.

The term *old* is a qualitative term. For dogs, as well as their masters, old is relative. Certainly we can all distinguish between a puppy Lowchen and an adult Lowchen—there are the obvious physical traits, such as size, appearance and facial expressions, and personality traits as well. Puppies and young dogs like to play with children. Children's natural exuberance is a good match for the seemingly endless energy of young dogs. They like to run, jump, chase and retrieve. When dogs grow older and cease their interaction with children, they are often thought of as being too old to play with the kids. On the other hand, if a Lowchen is only exposed to people over 60 years of age, its life will normally be less active and it will not seem to be getting old as its activity level slows down.

If people live to be 100 years old, dogs live to be 20 years old. While this is a good rule of thumb, it is very inaccurate. When trying to compare dog years to human years, you cannot make a generalisation about all dogs. You can make the generalisation

that 15 years is a good lifespan for a Lowchen, which is considered a long lifespan. Most small breeds enjoy longer lifespans than their large-breed counterparts. The Lowchen is considered mature at three years of age, but can reproduce even earlier. So the first three years of a dog's life are like seven times that of comparable humans. That means a 3-year-old dog is like a 21-year-old human. As the curve of comparison shows, there is no hard and fast rule for comparing dog and human ages. The comparison is made even more difficult, for not all humans age at the same rate...and human females live longer than human males.

WHAT TO LOOK FOR IN SENIORS
Most veterinary surgeons and behaviourists use the seventh year mark as the time to consider a dog a 'senior.' The term 'senior' does not imply that the dog is geriatric and has begun to fail in mind and body. Ageing is essentially a slowing process. Humans readily admit that they feel a difference in their activity level from age 20 to 30, and then from 30 to 40, etc.

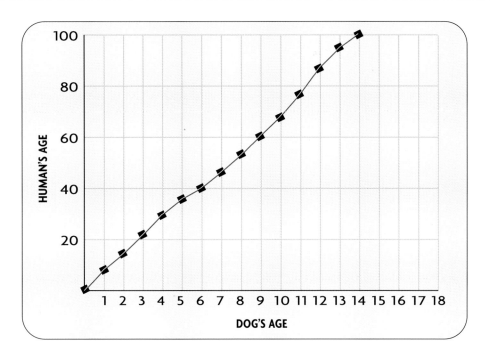

By treating the seven-year-old dog as a senior, owners are able to implement certain therapeutic and preventative medical strategies with the help of their veterinary surgeons. A senior-care programme should include at least two veterinary visits per year, screening sessions to determine the dog's health status, as well as nutritional counselling. Veterinary surgeons determine the senior dog's health status through a blood smear for a complete blood count, serum chemistry profile with electrolytes, urinalysis, blood pressure check, electrocardiogram, ocular tonometry (pressure on the eyeball) and dental prophylaxis.

Such an extensive programme for senior dogs is well advised before owners start to see the obvious physical signs of ageing, such as slower and inhibited movement, greying, increased sleep/nap periods and disinterest in play and other activity. This preventative programme promises a longer, healthier life for the ageing dog. Among the physical problems common in ageing dogs are the loss of sight and hearing, arthritis, kidney and liver failure, diabetes mellitus, heart disease and Cushing's disease (a hormonal disease).

In addition to the physical

manifestations discussed, there are some behavioural changes and problems related to ageing dogs. Dogs suffering from hearing or vision loss, dental discomfort or arthritis can become aggressive. Likewise the near-deaf and/or blind dog may be startled more easily and react in an unexpectedly aggressive manner. Seniors suffering from senility can become more impatient and irritable. Housesoiling accidents are associated with loss of mobility, kidney problems, loss of sphincter control as well as plaque accumulation, physiological brain changes and reactions to medications. Older dogs, just like young puppies, suffer from separation anxiety, which can lead to excessive barking, whining, housesoiling and destructive behaviour. Seniors may become fearful of everyday sounds, such as vacuum cleaners, heaters, thunder and passing traffic. Some dogs have difficulty sleeping, due to discomfort, the need for frequent toilet visits and the like.

Owners should avoid spoiling the older dog with too many fatty treats. Obesity is a common problem in older dogs and subtracts years from their lives. Keep the senior dog as trim as possible since excessive weight puts additional stress on the body's vital organs. Some breeders recommend supplementing the diet with foods high in fibre and lower in calories. Adding fresh vegetables and marrow broth to the senior's diet makes a tasty, low-calorie, low-fat supplement. Vets also offer speciality diets for senior dogs that are worth exploring.

Your dog, as he nears his twilight years, needs his owner's patience and good care more than ever. Never punish an older dog for an accident or abnormal behaviour. For all the years of love, protection and companionship that your dog has provided, he deserves special attention and courtesies. The older dog may need to relieve himself at 3 a.m. because he can no longer hold it for eight hours. Older dogs may not be able to remain crated for more than two or three hours. It may be time to give up a sofa or chair to your old friend. Although he may not seem as enthusiastic about your attention and petting, he does appreciate the considerations you offer as he gets older.

Your Lowchen does not understand why his world is slowing down. Owners must make the transition into the golden years as pleasant and rewarding as possible.

WHAT TO DO WHEN THE TIME COMES
You are never fully prepared to make a rational decision about putting your dog to sleep. It is very obvious that you love your Lowchen or you would not be

CDS
COGNITIVE DYSFUNCTION SYNDROME
'Old Dog Syndrome'

SYMPTOMS OF CDS

There are many ways to evaluate old-dog syndrome. Veterinary surgeons have defined CDS (cognitive dysfunction syndrome) as the gradual deterioration of cognitive abilities. These are indicated by changes in the dog's behaviour. When a dog changes its routine response, and maladies have been eliminated as the cause of these behavioural changes, then CDS is the usual diagnosis.

More than half the dogs over 8 years old suffer some form of CDS. The older the dog, the more chance it has of suffering from CDS. In humans, doctors often dismiss the CDS behavioural changes as part of 'winding down.'

There are four major signs of CDS: frequent toilet accidents inside the home, sleeps much more or much less than normal, acts confused, and fails to respond to social stimuli.

FREQUENT TOILET ACCIDENTS
- *Urinates in the house.*
- *Defecates in the house.*
- *Doesn't signal that he wants to go out.*

SLEEP PATTERNS
- *Moves much more slowly.*
- *Sleeps more than normal during the day.*
- *Sleeps less during the night.*

CONFUSION
- *Goes outside and just stands there.*
- *Appears confused with a faraway look in his eyes.*
- *Hides more often.*
- *Doesn't recognise friends.*
- *Doesn't come when called.*
- *Walks around listlessly and without a destination goal.*

FAILS TO RESPOND TO SOCIAL STIMULI
- *Comes to people less frequently, whether called or not.*
- *Doesn't tolerate petting for more than a short time.*
- *Doesn't come to the door when you return home from work.*

reading this book. Putting a loved dog to sleep is extremely difficult. It is a decision that must be made with your veterinary surgeon. You are usually forced to make the decision when one of the life-threatening symptoms listed above becomes serious enough for you to seek medical (veterinary) help.

If the prognosis of the malady indicates the end is near and your beloved pet will only suffer more and experience no enjoyment for the balance of its life, then euthanasia is the right choice.

WHAT IS EUTHANASIA?

Euthanasia derives from the Greek meaning *good death*. In other words, it means the planned, painless killing of a dog suffering from a painful, incurable condition, or who is so aged that it cannot walk, see, eat or control its excretory functions.

Euthanasia is usually accomplished by injection with an overdose of an anaesthesia or barbiturate. Aside from the prick of the needle, the experience is usually painless.

MAKING THE DECISION

The decision to euthanise your dog is never easy. The days during which the dog becomes ill and the end occurs can be unusually stressful for you. If this is your first experience with the death of a loved one, you may need the comfort dictated by your religious beliefs. If you are the head of the family and have children, you should have involved them in the decision of putting your Lowchen to sleep. Usually your dog can be maintained on drugs for a few days in order to give you ample time to make a decision. During this time, talking with members of your family or even people who have lived through this same experience can ease the burden of your inevitable decision.

THE FINAL RESTING PLACE

Dogs can have some of the same privileges as humans. The remains of your beloved dog can be buried in a pet cemetery, which is generally expensive. Dogs who have died at home can be buried in your garden in a place suitably marked with some stone or newly planted tree or bush. Alternatively, they can be cremated individually and the ashes returned to you. A less expensive option is mass cremation, although, of course, the ashes cannot then be returned.

EUTHANASIA
Euthanasia must be done by a licensed veterinary surgeon. There also may be societies for the prevention of cruelty to animals in your area. They often offer this service upon a vet's recommendation.

COPING WITH LOSS

When your dog dies, you may be as upset as when a human companion passes away. You are losing your protector, your baby, your confidante and best friend. Many people experience not only grief but also feelings of guilt and doubt as to whether they did all that they could for their pet. Allow yourself to grieve and mourn, and seek help from friends and support groups. You may also wish to consult books and websites that deal with this topic.

already developed personality. In this case, you can find out if you like each other after a few hours of being together.

The decision is, of course, your own. Do you want another Lowchen or perhaps a different breed so as to avoid comparison with your beloved friend? Most people usually buy the same breed because they know (and love) the characteristics of that breed. Then, too, they often know people who have the same breed and perhaps they are lucky enough that one of their friends expects a litter soon. What could be better?

Vets can usually arrange the cremation on your behalf. The cost of these options should always be discussed frankly and openly with your veterinary surgeon. In Britain if your dog has died at the surgery, the vet legally cannot allow you to take your dog's body home.

GETTING ANOTHER DOG?

The grief of losing your beloved dog will be as lasting as the grief of losing a human friend or relative. In most cases, if your dog died of old age (if there is such a thing), it had slowed down considerably. Do you want a new Lowchen puppy to replace it? Or are you better off finding a more mature Lowchen, say two to three years of age, which will usually be housetrained and will have an

Pet cemeteries usually can be found within reasonable distances from most well-populated areas.

When you purchased your Lowchen you should have made it clear to the breeder whether you wanted one just as a loveable companion and pet, or if you hoped to be buying a Lowchen with show prospects. No reputable breeder will sell you a young puppy saying that it is *definitely* of show quality, for so much can go wrong during the early months of a puppy's development. If you plan to show, what you will hopefully have acquired is a puppy with 'show potential.'

To the novice, exhibiting a Lowchen in the show ring may look easy but it takes a lot of hard work and devotion to do top winning at a show such as the prestigious Crufts, not to mention a little luck too!

The first concept that the canine novice learns when watching a dog show is that each dog first competes against members of its own breed. Once the judge has selected the best member of each breed, provided that the show is judged on a Group system, that chosen dog will compete with other dogs in its group. Finally the best of each group will compete for Best in Show and Reserve Best in Show.

The second concept that you must understand is that the dogs are not actually compared against one another. The judge compares each dog against the breed standard, which is a written description of the ideal specimen of the breed. While some early breed standards were indeed based on specific dogs that were famous or popular, many dedicated enthusiasts say that a perfect specimen, described in the standard, has never walked into a show ring, has never been bred and, to the woe of dog breeders around the globe, does not exist. Breeders attempt to get as close to this ideal as possible, with every litter, but theoretically the 'perfect' dog is so elusive that it is impossible. (And if the 'perfect' dog were born, breeders and judges would never agree that it was indeed 'perfect.')

If you are interested in exploring dog shows, your best bet is to join your local breed club. These clubs often host both Championship and Open Shows, and sometimes Match meetings and special events, all of which could be of interest, even if you are only an onlooker. Clubs also send out newsletters and some organise training days and seminars in order that people may learn more about their chosen breed. To locate the breed club closest to you, contact The Kennel Club, the ruling body for the British dog world. The Kennel Club governs not only conformation shows but also working trials, agility trials and field trials. The Kennel Club furnishes the rules and regulations for all these events plus general dog registration and other basic requirements of dog ownership. Its annual show, called the Crufts Dog Show, held in Birmingham, is the largest benched show in England. Every year over 20,000 of the UK's best dogs qualify to participate in this marvellous show which lasts four days.

The Kennel Club governs many different kinds of shows in Great Britain, Australia, South Africa and beyond. At the most competitive and prestigious of these shows, the Championship Shows, a dog can earn Challenge Certificates (CCs), and thereby become a Show Champion or a Champion. A dog must earn three Challenge Certificates under three different judges to earn the prefix of 'Sh Ch' or 'Ch.' Note that some breeds must also qualify in a field trial in order to gain the title of full champion. Challenge Certifi-

cates are awarded to a very small percentage of the dogs competing, and dogs that are already Champions compete with others for these coveted CCs. The number of Challenge Certificates

---

INFORMATION ON CLUBS
You can get information about dog shows from kennel clubs and breed clubs:

Fédération Cynologique Internationale
14, rue Leopold II,
B-6530 Thuin, Belgium
www.fci.be

The Kennel Club
1-5 Clarges St., Piccadilly,
London W1Y 8AB, UK
www.the-kennel-club.org.uk

American Kennel Club
5580 Centerview Dr.,
Raleigh, NC 27606-3390, USA
www.akc.org

Canadian Kennel Club
89 Skyway Ave., Suite 100,
Etobicoke, Ontario
M9W 6R4 Canada
www.ckc.ca

awarded in any one year is based upon the total number of dogs in each breed entered for competition.

There are three types of Championship Shows: an all-breed General Championship Show for all Kennel-Club-recognised breeds; a Group Championship Show, which is limited to breeds within one of the groups; and a Breed Show, which is usually confined to a single breed. The Kennel Club determines which breeds at which Championship Shows will have the opportunity to earn Challenge Certificates (or tickets). Serious exhibitors often will opt not to participate if the tickets are withheld at a particular show. This policy makes earning championships even more difficult to accomplish.

Open Shows are generally less competitive and are frequently used as 'practice shows' for young dogs. There are hundreds of Open Shows each year that can be delightful social events and are great first show experiences for the novice. Even if you're considering just watching a show to wet your paws, an Open Show is a great choice.

While Championship and Open Shows are most important for the beginner to understand, there are other types of shows in which the interested dog owner can participate. Training clubs

> **CLASSES AT DOG SHOWS**
> There can be as many as 18 classes per sex for your breed. Check the show schedule carefully to make sure that you have entered your dog in the appropriate class. Among the classes offered can be: Beginners; Minor Puppy (ages 6 to 9 months); Puppy (ages 6 to 12 months); Junior (ages 6 to 18 months); Beginners (handler or dog never won first place) as well as the following, each of which is defined in the schedule: Maiden; Novice; Tyro; Debutant; Undergraduate; Graduate; Post-graduate; Minor Limit; Mid Limit; Limit; Open; Veteran; Stud Dog; Brood Bitch; Progeny; Brace and Team.

sponsor Matches that can be entered on the day of the show for a nominal fee. In these introductory-level exhibitions, two dogs are pulled out of a hat and 'matched,' the winner of that match goes on to the next round, and eventually only one dog is left undefeated.

Exemption Shows are much more light-hearted affairs with usually only four pedigree classes and several 'fun' classes, all of which can be entered on that day. Exemption Shows are sometimes held in conjunction with small agricultural shows and the proceeds must be given to a charity. Limited Shows are also available in small number, but entry is restricted to members of the club which hosts the show, although one can usually join the club when making an entry.

Before you actually step into the ring, you would be well advised to sit back and observe the judge's ring procedure. If it is your first time in the ring, do not be over-anxious and run to the front of the line. It is much better to stand back and study how the exhibitor in front of you is performing. The judge asks each handler to 'stand' the dog, hopefully showing the dog off to his best advantage. The judge will observe the dog from a distance and from different angles, approach the dog, check his teeth, overall structure, alertness and muscle tone, as well as consider how well the dog 'conforms' to the standard. Most importantly, the judge will have the exhibitor move the dog around the ring in some pattern that he or she should specify (another advantage to not going first, but always listen since some judges change their directions, and the judge is always right!). Finally the judge will give the dog one last look before moving on to the next exhibitor.

If you are not in the top three at your first show, do not be discouraged. Be patient and consistent and you may eventu-

HOW TO ENTER A DOG SHOW
1. Obtain an entry form and show schedule from the Show Secretary.
2. Select the classes that you want to enter and complete the entry form.
3. Transfer your dog into your name at The Kennel Club. (Be sure that this matter is handled before entering.)
4. Find out how far in advance show entries must be made. Oftentimes it's more than a couple of months.

ally find yourself in the winning line-up. Remember that the winners were once in your shoes and have devoted many hours and much money to earn the placement. If you find that your dog is losing every time and never getting a nod, it may be time to consider a different dog sport or just enjoy your Lowchen as a pet.

WORKING TRIALS

Working trials can be entered by any well-trained dog of any breed, not just Gundogs or Working dogs.

Many dogs that earn the Kennel Club Good Citizen Dog award choose to participate in a working trial. There are five stakes at both open and championship levels: Companion Dog (CD), Utility Dog (UD), Working Dog (WD), Tracking Dog (TD) and Patrol Dog (PD). As in conformation shows, dogs compete against a standard and if the dog reaches the qualifying mark, it obtains a certificate. Divided into groups, each exercise must be achieved 70 percent in order for the dog to qualify. If the

The Lowchen is examined by the judge on a grooming table. Judges will thoroughly examine the dog's conformation, including its teeth, testicles and eyes.

TEMPERAMENT PLUS
Although it seems that physical conformation is the only factor considered in the show ring, temperament is also of utmost importance. An aggressive or fearful dog should not be shown, as bad behaviour will not be tolerated and may pose a threat to the judge, other exhibitors, you and your dog.

dog achieves 80 percent in the open level, it receives a Certificate of Merit (COM); in the championship level, it receives a Qualifying Certificate. At the CD stake, dogs must participate in four groups: Control, Stay, Agility and Search (Retrieve and Nosework). At the next three levels, UD, WD and TD, there are only three groups: Control, Agility and Nosework.

Agility consists of three jumps: a vertical scale up a wall of planks; a clear jump over a basic hurdle with a removable top bar; and a long jump across angled planks.

To earn the UD, WD and TD, dogs must track approximately one-half mile for articles laid from one-half hour to three hours previously. Tracks consist of turns and legs, and fresh ground is used for each participant. The fifth stake, PD, involves teaching manwork, which is not recommended for every breed.

AGILITY TRIALS
Agility trials began in the United Kingdom in 1977 and have since spread around the world, especially to the United States, where they are very popular. The handler directs his dog over an obstacle course that includes jumps (such as those used in the working trials), as well as tyres, the dog walk, weave poles, pipe tunnels, collapsed tunnels, etc. The Kennel Club requires that dogs not be trained for agility until they are 12 months old. Mini-agility was devised so that small breeds like the Lowchen would have the opportunity to participate in agility and compete in agility trials. This dog sport is great fun for dog and owner and interested owners should join a training club that has obstacles and experienced agility handlers who can introduce you and your dog to the 'ropes' (and tyres, tunnels, etc.).

FÉDÉRATION CYNOLOGIQUE INTERNATIONALE
Established in 1911, the Fédération Cynologique Internationale (FCI) represents the 'world kennel club.' This international body brings uniformity to the breeding, judging and showing of pure-bred dogs. Although the FCI originally included only five European nations: France, Germany, Austria, the Netherlands and Belgium (which remains its

headquarters), the organisation today embraces nations on six continents and recognises well over 300 breeds of pure-bred dog. There are three titles attainable through the FCI: the International Champion, which is the most prestigious; the International Beauty Champion, which is based on aptitude certificates in different countries; and the International Trial Champion, which is based on achievement in obedience trials in different countries. Dogs from every country can participate in these impressive canine spectacles, the largest of which is the World Dog Show, hosted in a different country each year. FCI sponsors both national and international shows. The hosting country determines the judging system and standards are always based on the breed's country of origin.

> **DID YOU KNOW?**
> The FCI *does not* issue pedigrees. The FCI members and contract partners are responsible for issuing pedigrees and training judges in their own countries. The FCI does maintain a list of judges and makes sure that they are recognised throughout the FCI member countries.
>
> The FCI also *does not* act as a breeder referral; breeder information is available from FCI-recognised national canine societies in each of the FCI's member countries.

A windy victory for these two Lowchens, posing with their handlers and the judge. Outdoor shows are popular, though inclement weather can make these events more challenging than an owner may expect.

speciality shows held by different breed clubs. Speciality shows may have their own regulations.

The FCI is divided into ten 'Groups.' At the World Dog Show, the following 'Classes' are offered for each breed: Puppy Class (6–9 months), Youth Class (9–18 months), Open Class (15 months or older) and Champion Class. A dog can be awarded a classification of Excellent, Very Good, Good, Sufficient and Not Sufficient. Puppies can be awarded classifications of Very Promising, Promising or Not Promising. Four placements are made in each class. After all sexes and classes are judged, a Best of Breed is selected. Other special groups and classes may also be shown. Each exhibitor showing a dog receives a written evaluation from the judge.

Besides the World Dog Show, you can exhibit your dog at

INDEX

*Page numbers in **boldface** indicate illustrations.*

My Lowchen

PUT YOUR PUPPY'S FIRST PICTURE HERE

Dog's Name _____

Date _____ Photographer _____